THE CATCHER—BASEBALL'S MAN IN CHARGE

THE CATCHER—BASEBALL'S MAN IN CHARGE

George Sullivan

Illustrated with photographs and diagrams

DODD, MEAD & COMPANY
New York

PICTURE CREDITS

Boston Red Sox, 13; California Angels, *frontispiece;* Detroit Tigers, 19, 20; Houston Astros, 36, 37; Los Angeles Dodgers, 18 (right); Montreal Expos, 21; National Baseball Hall of Fame & Museum, 73, 75, 77, 80 (right), 83, 85, 90, 92, 97, 98; New York Public Library, 70, 71, 72, 74, 76, 78, 79, 80 (left); Pittsburgh Pirates, 68; San Diego Padres, 24; San Francisco Giants (Dennis Desprois), 34; from the collection of Timothy Sullivan, 99, 100. All other photographs are by George Sullivan.

Frontispiece: **Angel's Ellie Rodriguez manages to hold the ball and make the tag in the fury of a play at home plate.**

Copyright © 1976 by George Sullivan
All rights reserved
No part of this book may be reproduced in any form without permission in writing from the publisher
Printed in the United States of America

Library of Congress Cataloging in Publication Data

Sullivan, George, 1927–
    The catcher—baseball's man in charge.

    1. Catching (Baseball)—Juvenile literature. 2. Catchers (Baseball)—Biography—Juvenile literature.
I. Title.
GV872.S78   796.357'23   75-37650
ISBN 0-396-07278-X

ACKNOWLEDGMENTS

The author is grateful to the many people who assisted him by providing source material and photographs for use in this book. Special thanks are offered John Redding, Librarian, National Baseball Library of the National Baseball Hall of Fame and Museum; Marty Appel, Publicity Director, Clyde Kluttz, Special Assignment Scout, and Coach Elston Howard of the New York Yankees, and the New York Public Library for the opportunity to consult the A. G. Spalding Collection of historical data. The author is also grateful to Herb Field, Herb Field Art Studios; Gary Wagner, Wagner International Photos; Larry Shenk, Philadelphia Phillies; Hal Middlesworth, Detroit Tigers; George Lederer, California Angels; Bill Crowley, Boston Red Sox; Larry Chiasson, Montreal Expos; Art Santo Domingo, San Francisco Giants; Bobby Risinger, Houston Astros; and William Guilfoile, Pittsburgh Pirates.

CONTENTS

The Era of the Catcher	9	The Best	83
What It Takes	23	Supercatcher	102
Running the Ball Game	39	You're the Catcher	114
Stop, Thief!	60	Index	121
Looking Back	70		

Johnny Bench—*outstanding in everything a catcher has to do.*

THE ERA OF THE CATCHER

This was a game early in Johnny Bench's career. The Reds were playing the Dodgers.

Ron Fairly, leading off for the Dodgers in the sixth inning, banged out a double. The next batter, Tom Haller, was instructed to sacrifice to move Fairly to third. Bench diagnosed what was afoot and called for a low outside curve, which Haller couldn't reach. Fairly was four steps off second when he realized that Haller had missed the ball, and whirled and dived back to the base. Too late! Bench's throw nailed him. One out.

After Haller walked, Teddy Davidson uncorked a wild pitch. Bench pursued the ball all the way to the backstop, trapped it while on one knee, and without rising, gunned the ball to third to nip Haller sliding in. Two outs.

The next batter placed a perfect bunt down the first-base line. Bench sprang and threw a bullet to first to get the runner by six steps. Three outs. Three Johnny Bench outs.

The fact that the Cincinnati Reds have been one of the standout teams in the National League in recent years is no accident. The reason wears No. 5 on his back and squats behind the plate.

There is no argument that in any given game the pitcher is the most important man on the field, and what he does—or fails to do—affects the game's outcome more than anything else. But over the course of a season, a solid catcher is a much more valuable player. Because he is required to do so many things, the catcher, too, has a sharp influence on how the game is decided. And not occasionally—not in one game out of every four or five, like the pitcher—but day after day after day. Most front-line catchers play in from 140 to 150 games a season.

"You never see a good ball club with a poor catcher," says a baseball official. "Nor do you ever see a poor club with a good catcher."

It's not difficult to understand why this is true. The catcher is something like the conductor of an orchestra. He has to know what each man is capable of doing, especially his star performer, the pitcher, and threaten, wheedle, or cajole excellence out of each one.

But being canny and intelligent is not enough. He also has to be big, strong, and agile. He has to be aggressive. He has to be durable.

Indeed, durability is one of the first qualities that scouts look for. Catching a game is similar to jaywalking in heavy traffic. Sooner or later, you're going to get hurt. The catcher has to be able to withstand foul tips that smash into his mask and endure those bone-jarring collisions at home plate. His toes and fingertips are always getting nicked. As Ray Fosse, who did the catching for the Oakland A's, once expressed it, "A catcher who doesn't get hurt has had a good year."

Fosse has to be considered an expert on the subject. A fine rookie catcher with the Cleveland Indians in 1970, Fosse was catching in the All-Star game that year when Pete Rose came barreling toward home plate with what he hoped was the winning run. Fosse took the throw from the outfield, turned to make the tag, and Rose slammed into him as if he were clearing the way for O. J. Simpson. Fosse let the ball get away and Rose scored.

The worst was yet to come. Fosse came out of the collision with a sore shoulder and the inability to swing the bat normally. He saw his average fall 40 points and the next season he continued to be anemic at the plate. Then it was discovered that Fosse had broken his shoulder when Rose plowed into him.

After Fosse's average slipped to .241 in 1972, Cleveland traded him to Oakland. "I haven't been the same since that All-Star game," Fosse reflected in 1974. "I figure it cost me at least two years of hitting."

Fosse also had the index finger of his right hand broken three seasons in a row, and he fractured a thumb. He was struck in the throat with a foul tip and while batting was hit on the leg by one of Nolan Ryan's fastballs. No wonder that Fosse says, "A catcher who doesn't get hurt has had a good year."

Durability also implies the willingness to spend two or three hours of every working day in a tortuous crouch. It's been estimated that a catcher squats about 200 times in the average game. His thighs and calves often develop painful knots. On summer afternoons sweat runs down his face from behind the mask. His uniform becomes sweat-stained and grimy. His arm aches from all that throwing.

Up until fairly recent times, outstanding receivers (a word that players and managers like to use) were about as rare as rainouts in Los Angeles. Good catchers have always seemed to run in cycles. The 1930s were the time of Mickey Cochrane, Gabby Hartnett, and Bill Dickey, all of whom were exceptional. The 1950s had Yogi Berra, Roy Campanella, and then Elston Howard. More greatness.

While most catchers of the 1960s were dependable, their talent seldom went beyond that level. "If your kid wants to become a major league ball player, teach him to catch," scouts were fond of saying during this period. "Every team needs catchers."

What happened is apparent to even the most casual of fans. Just about every team of the present day is well fortified behind the plate.

What has come to be known as "The Era of the Catcher" began in 1968, the year that twenty-two-year-old Johnny Bench was named the National League's Rookie of the Year. Never before in baseball history had the honor gone to a catcher. (Bench is profiled in depth in a later chapter.)

That was merely the beginning. Bench, through

1974, had won the National League's Golden Glove award as the best fielding catcher seven times in his first eight seasons. Year in and year out, he was a member of the All-Star team and more often than not he was in the starting lineup. When the fans voted their All-Star selections in 1974, only Hank Aaron got more votes than Johnny. He was the first catcher in the history of the game to earn in excess of $100,000 a year.

No one has ever hinted that Bench isn't worth every cent he's paid. "He just does things that other catchers can't do," says Cincinnati manager Sparky Anderson. "He'll grab a ball that's inside and be in a throwing motion at the same time. He has a way of fielding a bunt in front of the plate so that as he picks it up, he's bounding back to throw. And he makes the play at the plate better than anyone. He just takes the plate away from the runner."

Bench has an exceptional arm; he terrorizes base runners. And he's a strong hitter, an excellent clutch hitter.

It is Bench more than any other catcher who has perfected and popularized the one-hand style of catching in vogue today. This involves the use of a mitt with a deep crease, a kind of hinge, built into the heel. The hinge makes it easy to fold the glove sides together, the way you might fold over a slice of bread to make a sandwich. It's the hinged mitt that enables a catcher to reach out and snare the ball with one hand.

The traditional catcher's mitt, round as a dinner plate, had no fold in the rim. You had to use your right hand to keep the ball from popping out. Sure, the right hand got in the way of the pitch now and then, but that was considered one of the hazards of the occupation.

Randy Hundley, who became a regular with the Chicago Cubs in 1966 after five years of minor league experience, is credited with being the catcher who pioneered in the use of the one-handed glove. When the pitch came plateward, Hundley would protect his bare hand behind the glove or outside his right knee.

Johnny Bench learned to catch in the classic two-hand manner. But after he broke a thumb in the minor leagues, he switched to the hinged mitt, and quickly became a virtuoso in its use. After gloving the ball, he sweeps it over quickly to his bare hand, actually turning it so he can grab it across the seams for the throw.

Over in the American League, it's generally agreed that the catcher with the most natural ability is Thurman Munson of the New York Yankees. He has amazingly quick hands and a fast release. At the plate, he's a powerful pull hitter.

Munson is confident, even cocky. Some of his teammates once spread the story that the Yankees and the Cincinnati Reds had completed a spectacular deal, one that was to bring Johnny Bench to the Yankees.

"Bench? Coming here?" said Munson. "Great! But where's he gonna play? Designated hitter?"

Munson, who was born and grew up in Canton, Ohio, was an all-around athlete in high school. He played linebacker for the high school football team, was a guard on the basketball team (and once made an All-County team), and, in baseball, a shortstop and second baseman. Not until his senior year did he try his hand at catching.

Munson received scholarship offers from countless colleges. But they were all for football—all but one, that is. Kent State offered him a baseball scholarship. Munson went to Kent State.

Not long after he had won college All-American honors, the Yankees drafted him, and then sent him to the minor leagues for seasoning. Munson played 71 games for Binghamton in the Eastern League. The Yankees decided that was enough, and brought him up to the majors.

Munson, at twenty-eight, after five seasons as a member of the New York Yankees, could look back on some splendid achievements. In 1970, his first year with the team, he batted .302 and was the American League's Rookie of the Year. In 1971, he led all catchers in fielding, although his batting average slipped to .251. In 1972, he hit .280; in 1973, .305. Injuries hampered him in 1974, but the following season was his best at the plate, as he hit .318, fourth highest in the American League. All in all, he's done much to uphold a Yankee tradition for excellence behind the plate, a tradition established by Bill Dickey and carried forward by Yogi Berra and Elston Howard.

Beginning in 1972, Munson, a perennial All-Star choice, began to have a rival for such honors. That was the year that Boston's twenty-four-year-old

Yankees' Thurman Munson is quick and confident, packs power at the plate.

Carlton Fisk of the Red Sox is cool as he tags out Norm Cash.

Without Fisk, Red Sox Could Be Dead Sox

Headline from *The Sporting News* gives evidence of Fisk's value.

Carlton Fisk won Rookie of the Year honors. Not only did Fisk establish himself as a splendid defensive catcher, he also won acclaim as one of baseball's fine young hitters.

Aggressiveness was Fisk's dominant characteristic. He was involved in frequent collisions at home plate. He had fist fights with Thurman Munson and California's Alan Gallagher. "He's got a lot to learn," Frank Robinson once said of Fisk.

While Fisk would never win a popularity contest among opposing players, with fans of the Red Sox it was a much different story. The huge souvenir shop across the street from Fenway Park stocks as many color photographs of Fisk as it does of veteran Carl Yastrzemski, long the favorite of New England fans. This isn't hard to understand, considering that Fisk was born in Vermont, in Bellows Falls, and brought up across the state line in Charlestown, New Hampshire. Both states now claim him.

The only thing that has prevented Fisk from becoming the greatest thing in New England since codfish cakes is an injury jinx. He suffered a separated shoulder in his last year in the minors. Midway in his third season with the Red Sox, he was involved in a collision at home plate with Loren Lee of the Cleveland Indians in which he tore ligaments in his left knee. Surgery to repair the damage quickly followed, and Fisk was sidelined for the rest of the year.

Fisk worked "incredibly hard," according to the Red Sox trainer, to regain full use of the leg. His regimen included lifting weights and running two and a half miles every morning.

In spring training the following season, the hex struck again. At bat, facing Detroit's Fred Holdsworth, Fisk was struck by a pitch that fractured his left forearm. Months of inactivity followed. Nevertheless, Fisk still managed to hit .331 in 1975, and he belted a home run in helping the Red Sox win the dramatic sixth game of the World Series. But his injury record has cast a shadow over Fisk's bright future.

No such misfortunes have hampered the career of Mannie Sanguillen of the Pittsburgh Pirates. Indeed, the popular Sanguillen is one of the most durable of catchers. In one stretch during the 1974 season, he played in 93 of the Pirates' 94 games, and appeared in 151 for the year.

He rarely ever complained of aches and pains. It was said that whenever he went into the trainer's room, it was only to rib whichever of his teammates happened to be on the rubbing table.

Sanguillen, who entered major league baseball a year after Johnny Bench, has more speed than the Cincinnati receiver and usually hits for a higher average. He is reminiscent of Yogi Berra in that he is a dangerous bad-ball hitter. In a game against the Cardinals, Sanguillen once rapped out five hits. "We didn't throw him a single pitch in the strike zone," catcher Ted Simmons moaned afterward.

In his first seven major league seasons, Sanguillen never went below .280, and he was above .300 several times. In terms of consistency at the plate, no other catcher in recent history has been the equal of Sanguillen.

He has first-rate ability *behind* the plate, too. "From my point of view," says pitcher Dave Giusti, "Sangy is really in control out there. Physically, he's an acrobat. He can scramble for a low pitch in the dirt better than anyone I've ever seen. He's got a great arm, great legs, great wrists and reflexes. And he uses his head."

The St. Louis Cards are strong in catching, thanks to the presence of tough and durable Ted Simmons. One of the best hitting catchers in baseball, Simmons averaged over .300 in each of his first three seasons with the team, a rare accomplishment. Simmons is helped by the fact that he's a switch-hitter.

Simmons received a $50,000 bonus for signing with the Cards in 1967, but it was largely because he could hit the ball consistently and for distance. As a defensive catcher, he had a poor reputation.

"But he worked hard," says Cardinal coach

Pirates' Manny Sanguillen gets high marks for durability.

George Kissell. "He strengthened his arm by throwing daily in the outfield, from right field to left, then from left to right."

During the 1974 season, Joe Torre, then a teammate of Simmons and a former catcher himself, said of Simmons, "He's still not the smoothest catcher, but he gets the job done. He's about as strong as any human being I've seen, and he has all the leadership qualities."

The Philadelphia Phillies boast a top-flight receiver in quiet, unassuming Bob Boone. Tall and rangy, Boone was a twenty-three-year-old third baseman at Raleigh-Durham when, in 1971, the Phillies asked him to take over behind the plate. After another year of minor league seasoning, Boone became the Phillies' starting catcher.

Bob is a graduate of Stanford, where he earned a B.A. degree in psychology. But he says that what he learned at college was not of great help to him in becoming a regular. Of more value was the schooling he received at the Phillies' farm club in Eugene, Oregon, where Andy Seminick, a former catcher, was the manager.

"Seminick was tough. He was on me all the time," says Boone. "Maybe he wouldn't have been so hard if he hadn't been a catcher. But looking back, it was a godsend for me."

What are Boone's attributes? He has good hands,

Ted Simmons is tough, a fine switch-hitter.

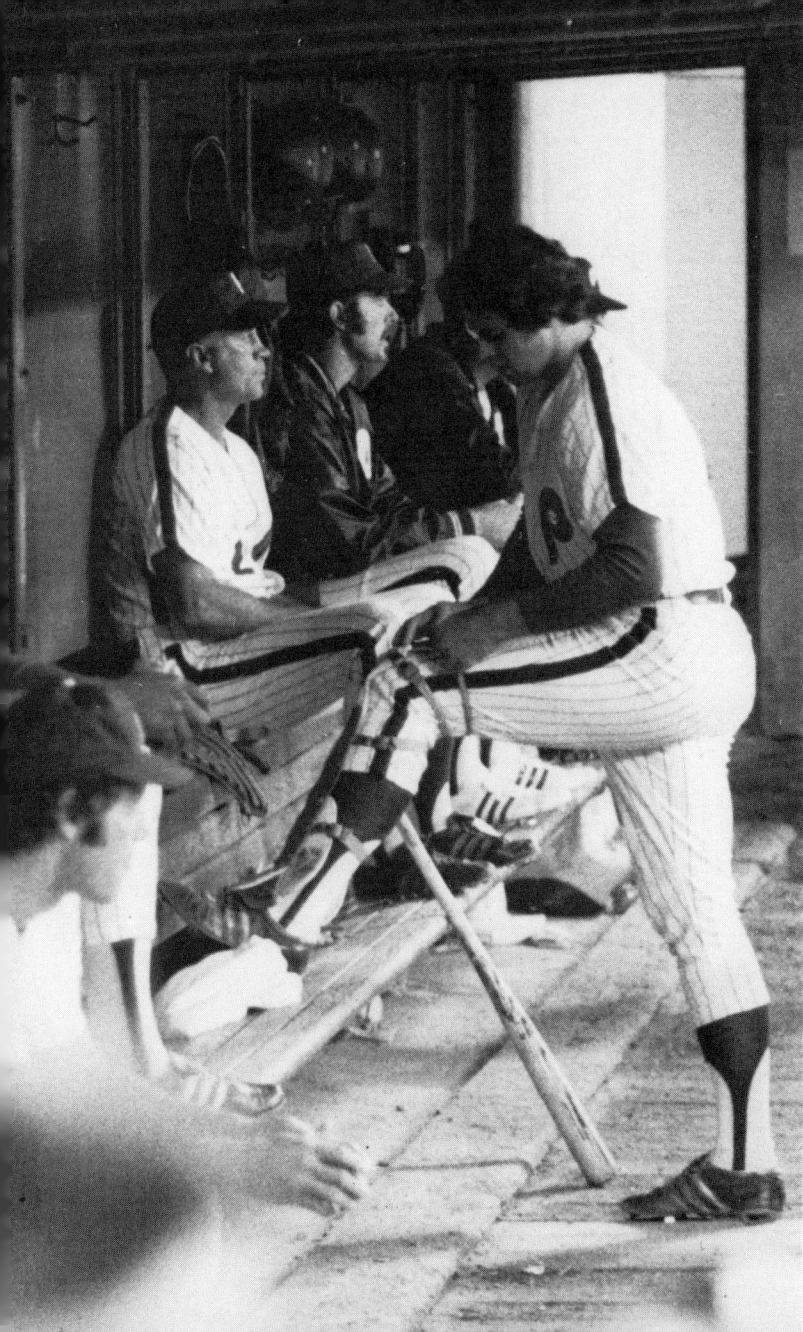

a good arm, a quick mind, and he can hit.

The Los Angeles Dodgers have had not merely one outstanding catcher, but two of them—Steve Yeager and Joe Ferguson. Yeager was regarded as the better defensive catcher of the two, while Ferguson gained renown as a power hitter. In an effort to get Ferguson into the lineup when Yeager was behind the plate, the Dodgers often used him as a right fielder against left-handed pitching.

Yeager felt that in some respects he was a better catcher than Johnny Bench. "We both have strong arms," Yeager once told Bob Oates of the Los Angeles *Times*. "But I block the low pitch better than he does.

"And I work harder. I have to," he added, "because Bench is a better hitter."

One other catcher of recent times must be mentioned—Bill Freehan of the Detroit Tigers. For year-in, year-out excellence, few catchers have been Freehan's equal. He also earned a four-star rating for durability. In 1974 he completed his tenth consecutive season of catching 100 or more games. The record in this department, thirteen consecutive seasons, is held by Bill Dickey of the New York Yankees.

Freehan looked like what you want a catcher to look like. He stood 6-feet-3; he weighed 210. He looked like he might be the boss of a construction

Phillies' Bob Boone gets ready.

Joe Ferguson gives Los Angeles punch at the plate.

Left: **Dodgers' Steve Yeager** is well known for his defensive skills.

crew, and he would not be out of place as a Marine drill instructor. If Freehan had played pro football, he'd have been a linebacker, a hitter, a deadly hitter.

Born and raised in Highland Park, Michigan, which is within Detroit itself, Freehan played sandlot baseball well enough to win a scholarship to the University of Michigan. In his sophomore year he batted .485, a Big Ten record, and scouts began jamming the highways to Ann Arbor. After he graduated, Freehan signed with the Tigers because they promised him a big bonus—over $100,000—and because the team needed catching.

The Detroit management planned to school Freehan in the minor leagues for three or four years.

When batting, Freehan attacked the ball.

Freehan excelled in plays at home plate.

But his rapid progress convinced them to cut the training period in half, and by 1963 Freehan was wearing a Detroit uniform on a full-time basis.

The following year he blossomed, becoming the first Detroit catcher since Mickey Cochrane to hit .300. He also displayed remarkable stamina. In one stretch that season, he caught 446 innings without relief, the equivalent of 49 games. He was named to the league's All-Star squad, becoming, at twenty-three, the youngest catcher ever selected.

For most of the decade that followed, Freehan was the dominant catcher in the American League, and some observers said the dominant player in the game. He won such praise, not merely because of his skill as a batter, nor his fine fielding, which saw him win five Golden Glove awards; nor was it by virtue of his versatility, although he was not reluctant to take over as either a first baseman or outfielder. He was named to the league's All-Star team year in and year out, but that wasn't what made him preeminent, either.

Freehan became dominant because he was the Tigers' boss. He took charge of the game and ran it.

When Freehan blocked the plate to a runner careening in from third base, he really blocked it. "Running into Freehan," said one player who had tried it, "is like running into a freight train."

Expos' Barry Foote has been described as "the next Johnny Bench."

Darrell Porter of the Brewers has bright future, say the experts.

When at the plate with a bat in his hand, Freehan displayed a short, fierce swing. He attacked the ball. Called strikes were not for Bill Freehan.

Like all players, he thrived on base hits, but his greatest enjoyment was to call a shutout. "You can go four-for-four," he once said, "and the team can beat you. But when you call a shutout, there's no way you can lose."

During the mid-1970s, Freehan and other established stars began to become aware of a new generation of catching talent, young stars on the rise.

There were several of them. Milt May of the Detroit Tigers and Jim Sundberg of the Texas Rangers were spoken of in glowing terms. "The next Johnny Bench" was the way that Gene Mauch, manager of the Montreal Expos, described his catcher, Barry Foote.

Dave Rader of the San Francisco Giants, Darrell Porter of the Milwaukee Brewers, and Steve Swisher of the Chicago Cubs were other receivers who were being hailed for their all-around ability. Catching's future seems in good hands.

Hustle—catcher Buck Martinez hurries to first base to back up the play.

WHAT IT TAKES

Catching is the toughest position in baseball. As such, it demands a special kind of player.

A young catching prospect, like any other player, is evaluated on a wide assortment of things—on the strength and accuracy of his throwing arm, his running speed, hitting ability, and fielding ability. The matter of attitude, important in every young prospect, is crucial to catching.

"A catcher really has to want to play, want to catch," says Clyde Kluttz, a special assignment scout for the New York Yankees. "A good catcher is always doing something—warming up a pitcher or catching batting practice. And he has to have the desire to do these things; he has to enjoy doing them. If he doesn't he'll never become a major league catcher."

Many scouts say that a player's attitude is the most difficult of all qualities to judge. "You can't cut them open and see what they're made of" is a scouting adage.

In an effort to find out how much desire a prospect has, how much determination, a scout will watch carefully from the moment the player steps out onto the field. How does the young man go about getting his job done? How does he relate to

CLUB REPORT FORM – PROFESSIONAL															

Club_____ League_____ Manager/Coach_____

Organization_____ Dates Scouted_____ Reported by_____

A+ — MAJOR LEAGUE—Superior
A — MAJOR LEAGUE—Average
A− — MAJOR LEAGUE—Below Average
B+ — FAIR—Needs Slight Improvement
B — FAIR—Needs More Improvement
B− — FAIR—Needs Great Improvement
C — POOR—No Prospect in this Area

Catchers, Infielders, Outfielders	Pos.	Age	Race	Ht.	Wt.	B	T	HITTING		Spd.	Arm	Fld.	Mil. Cl.	Class/Draft Status	Top Class	Class To Play Next Year
								Abil.	Pow.							

Young prospects are graded in several categories on a scale ranging from A+ (superior) to C (poor).

his teammates? Is he a leader? Does he take charge? If he doesn't have leadership qualities at an early age, it's not likely that he will ever develop them.

The scout will talk with the young man. He'll talk to the player's manager, his teammates, and friends. He'll get opinions from other scouts. He'll visit his school. What kind of student is he? Does he participate in school activities? The scout will visit the boy's home and talk to his parents.

"What's really discouraging," says one scout, "is to see a kid who has the talent to play major league baseball, but he doesn't have the right attitude; he doesn't seem to care. He's usually a natural athlete, and everything has come easy for him. But he'd rather have his fun off the field than work at developing his potential. It's kind of sad."

To be a catcher, a player must have stamina and be durable. How do you judge these qualities in a young player? "You look for strength," says Clyde Kluttz. "You follow him into the shower room and you look for heavily muscled legs. You look for a strong back."

A catching prospect must also demonstrate strength in his throwing arm. "If he can't throw hard," says Kluttz, once a major league catcher himself, "he'll never make it as a catcher."

Speed on the basepaths is also a factor, although it is less important with a catching prospect than it is with other players. Each scout is equipped with a stopwatch to time how long it takes a player to reach first base from the time his bat smacks the ball. For a right-handed hitter, 4.3 seconds is the

Catchers of the 1970s are often tall and slim—like Carlton Fisk.

average time to first base. For a left-handed hitter, it's 4.2 seconds. A time of 4.1 seconds is considered excellent.

When a scout discovers a fine catcher who also hits the ball well, he's made a real find. Catchers usually aren't good hitters.

All that squatting behind the plate takes its toll. Johnny Bench says catchers usually aren't good hitters because catching itself "is a little rougher job. Those foul tips keep banging you around."

But there's another reason, certainly just as important. "A lot of times you don't get to think about what the pitcher's throwing," says Bench, "or how he's going to work on you until you're in the on-deck circle. If I'm playing the outfield, I can think about all that. Guys like [Rusty] Staub, [Joe] Morgan, and [Pete] Rose make themselves good hitters because of their concentration."

How many catchers have led their leagues in batting? Johnny Bench never has (not as of 1975, anyway), nor Thurman Munson, nor Carlton Fisk.

Don't say it's Joe Torre, either. Torre, who broke into the major leagues as a catcher with the Milwaukee Braves in 1961, and was traded to St. Louis in 1969, did indeed win a batting title in 1971, but by that time he was an infielder, a third baseman. He hit .363 that year. When Torre was traded to the

New York Mets in 1975, it was for use as a third baseman, and the fact that he once had been a catcher had all but been forgotten.

Eugene (Bubbles) Hargrave, who started his major league career with the Chicago Cubs in 1913, and starred for the Cincinnati Reds during the 1920s, was the first catcher ever to lead the league in batting. He did it in 1926 with a .353 average. His lifetime average was a sparkling .312.

The only other catcher who managed to finish the season with an average higher than everyone else in the league was Ernie Lombardi, and Lombardi, incredibly, won the batting title, not once, but twice. Lombardi spent most of his career with the Cincinnati Reds, but he also caught for three other National League teams—Brooklyn, Boston, and New York.

Lombardi batted a league-leading .342 in 1938, a year he won the National League's Most Valuable Player award. His .330 in 1942 was his other league-leading effort.

In the ten years he wore the Reds' uniform, there was no other catcher quite Lombardi's equal. He had a way of making the ball give off a resounding "pop" when it hit into his glove, a bit of cunning that often got the pitcher to believe that he had more "stuff" on the ball than he actually did have.

You have to be strong-armed, too. This is Thurman Munson.

With his confidence thus boosted, he became a better pitcher.

Lombardi ended his career with a .306 lifetime batting average. Only a small handful of catchers have done as well.

It used to be that catchers were always short and stocky, built like granite blocks. Not any more. To be tall and rangy is more of the style today. Carlton Fisk of the Boston Red Sox, at 6-feet-2, 210 pounds, typifies the catcher of the 1970s. And then there is Fran Healy of the Kansas City Royals. Healy is 6-feet-5.

The fact that the major leagues expanded to twenty-four teams not long ago—twelve teams in the American League, twelve in the National—has created much more of a demand for young players than ever before. Is used to be that scouts would never attend a high school game and were seldom seen at college contests. But there have been cases in the last few years where high school players have made the jump to major league baseball, and at college games today it's often that a high percentage of the spectators are major league scouts.

In the case of catchers, the demand is especially acute. This is because more and more teams are carrying three catchers on their rosters—and nine pitchers. That's a 50 per cent increase; the "old" formula was two catchers and ten pitchers.

The No. 1 man does the bulk of the work, of course. The second man is the back-up catcher, used

Fran Healy unlimbers his 6-foot-5 frame.

Rick Dempsey (46) and Ed Herrmann handled back-up catching for the Yankees.

to handle the second game of a doubleheader or when the No. 1 man needs rest. The third catcher is for emergency use. "I keep three catchers," says Earl Weaver, manager of the Baltimore Orioles, "so that I can pinch-hit for a catcher whenever I want. And a broken finger won't ruin us."

Being the No. 2 man is no easy job. He has to be able to go into the game when needed, and be physically and mentally prepared to do the best job possible. The ability to hit is usually not a necessity with the back-up catcher; he's primarily a defensive specialist.

Staying in shape can be something of a problem with the No. 2 catcher. He has to work at it, warming up pitchers in the bullpen, or catching batting practice once in a while.

He can't let the fact that he's merely a substitute affect his mental attitude. "You have to learn to accept your status," says one, "and the fact that you can't do anything about it."

"Take charge of the ball after it's thrown," is what one manager tells his young catchers. "Never let the ball take charge of you."

Taking charge of the ball means meeting it with the mitt and catching it surely before it breaks out of the strike zone. This shouldn't imply that the catcher should fight the pitch in his eagerness to glove it. Instead, he should catch it with "soft hands." This refers to the ability to gather in the

With his hinged type mitt, Thurman Munson snares the ball with one hand.

pitch the way a football receiver snares a long pass.

This advice applies no matter what type of glove the catcher uses—the glove with the break, the hinge in the rim (as mentioned earlier), or the no-break type. The majority of catchers today favor the hinged type glove, and they catch the ball with one hand.

Carlton Fisk started using the one-hand style in 1972. "It really has helped me," he says. "I'd always used a catcher's mitt with no break in it. Then I changed to a more flexible mitt, and I found I was able to pick up low pitches easily with it.

"It also helped me with my throwing. You can get more on your throws."

Jim Hegan, a coach for the Detroit Tigers during the mid-1970s, and with eighteen years experience as a major league catcher, favored the no-break type of glove. It was no accident that the Tigers' Bill Freehan used one.

"The old-fashioned glove, the one without any break, is better for handling pitches that are knee-high to the batter," said Hegan. "You make the catch with your fingers pointing down, lifting the ball into the strike zone as you do. This can't help but affect the umpire's call.

"But you can't catch a knee-high pitch that way with the hinged type glove. The ball shoots right out through the break.

"What you have to do is face the glove pocket toward the ground, and slap down at the ball to

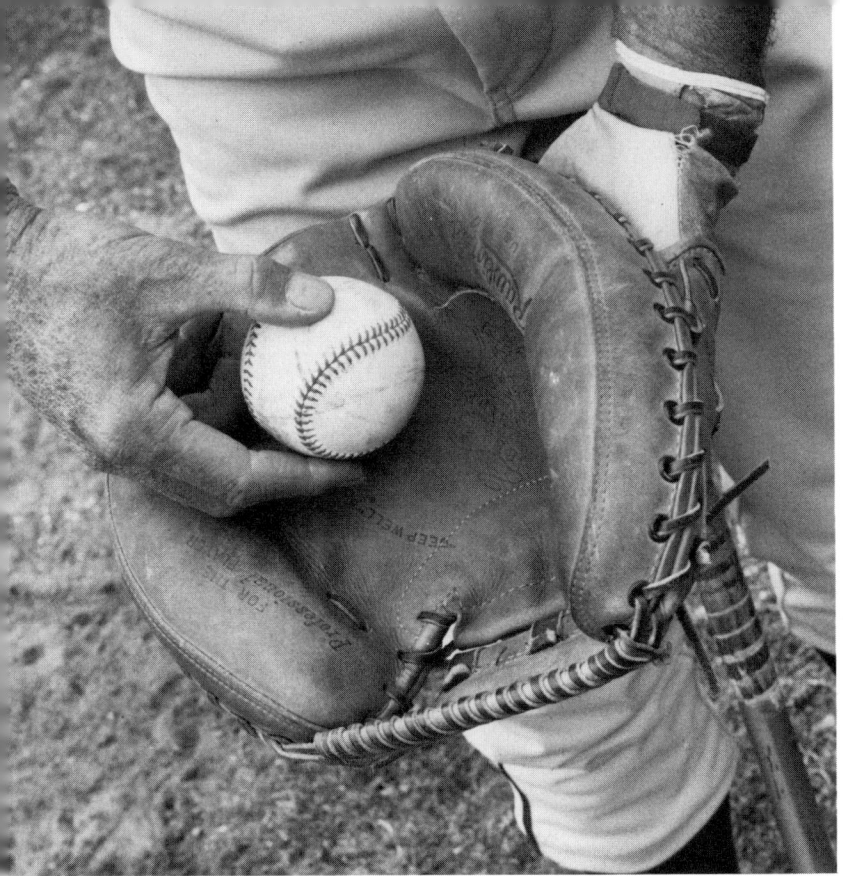

Coach Jim Hegan shows one disadvantage of the hinged type mitt. If the glove is held with the palm facing up, the ball can escape through the break on low pitches.

make the catch. So you end up taking the ball *out* of the strike zone, and you're going to lose some strikes as a result."

Hegan also said that the no-break glove was better because the catcher could get the ball out of the pocket quicker. "The bare hand is right there to grab the ball and make the throw," he said.

Del Crandall, former manager of the Milwaukee Brewers, and for years a top-flight catcher in the National League, preferred that his catchers use the no-break glove. Darrell Porter, the Brewers' No. 1 catcher, switched from the hinged glove to the no-break type at Crandall's urging. He soon came to prefer it. "Instead of reaching for the ball with one hand," he says, "you get your entire body in front of it, which is the safer way to make the catch. The other glove makes you lazy."

Despite these seeming disadvantages, the hinged type glove continues to grow in popularity, and not only among major league players, but among Little Leaguers as well. "It's the Johnny Bench influence," says a salesman for an equipment company. "Kids see Bench using the glove with the break, so that's the type they go out and buy. We don't sell many of the no-break kind any more."

One other type of mitt must be mentioned, and that's the oversize mitt that catchers use to handle the erratic offerings of knuckleball pitchers. To say that one of these mitts looks about the same size as a manhole cover is exaggerating, but not much. Such mitts can be either the break or no-break type.

They even look big to the players, especially the opposing players. In a game between the Mets and

Dodgers at Shea Stadium a few years ago, the New York batters chased the Los Angeles starting pitcher, and knuckleballer Charlie Hough came in to relieve. Dodger catcher Steve Yeager immediately switched to an outsize glove.

The Mets took one look and screamed in protest to umpire Tom Gorman, charging that the mitt was bigger than the rules permitted. "Not so," said Gorman, who happened to have a tape measure handy. "The rules allow a glove that is 38 inches

Manufacturers keep major league catchers well supplied with mitts. These belong to Bob Boone of the Phillies.

Catchers for the Atlanta Braves use the larger glove with the bigger pocket to catch knuckleball pitches of Phil Niekro. Standard mitt is at left.

in circumference. Yeager's is only 34½ inches. It's legal."

Even with the oversize mitt, no catcher ever really masters the art of gloving knuckleballs. They do weird things as they come shooting in. The Chicago White Sox had one of the best knuckleballers in baseball in Wilbur Wood, known as the man with "The Pitch of 1,000 Dances." Wood's catcher was Ed Herrmann. "What's the secret of catching a knuckleball?" Herrmann was once asked. "It's the same secret as hitting it," Herrmann answered. "Pray a lot."

Low pitches that bounce into the dirt are another problem. A good catcher will get down into the dirt and dig them out. A pitcher who is confident of his catcher's ability to do this is likely to be a much more effective pitcher. For one thing, he won't hesitate about firing a curveball (a pitch that breaks downward) when there are runners on the bases.

Who should make the play? Where should he throw? Catcher Paul Casanova has to decide.

High bounces cause difficulty, too. It's easy for one to carom off the catcher's chest protector, bouncing to either the left or right, while the runners all advance a base.

This won't happen, though, if the catcher keeps his body in front of the ball, bending from the waist slightly so as to put his chest (and his chest protector) at a slight angle with the ground. When the ball slams into his chest, it will rebound onto the ground in front of him, and he can pounce on it and make the throw.

The catcher's ability as a field general is put to the test any time a bunt is attempted. It's up to the catcher to decide who is to make the play and which base the throw should go to. After all, the infielders are charging toward the plate, their backs to the base runners. If the catcher doesn't make the throw himself, he shouts instructions to the man who gloves the ball.

In situations where a bunt attempt is almost certain, the catcher adjusts his stance slightly, putting his rear foot back farther than normal. This stance, similar to a sprinter's starting stance, enables him to break quickly for the ball once it's bunted.

If it's the catcher's ball to field, he darts forward, blocks it with his glove, and picks it up with the other hand. Of course, he can grab the ball barehanded right away, but more than a few managers

Giants' Dave Rader chases down a foul pop.

feel that stopping the ball with the glove first is the best procedure. That way the catcher is picking up a dead ball, and there's much less chance that he'll muff it. The throw to the base is overhand.

In going after a pop fly behind the plate, catchers are often instructed to "play the area." This means that the catcher should first sight the general area where the ball is going to come down, and run toward it, keeping an eye on the ball as he goes. Once he reaches the area, he should judge precisely where the ball is going to land, then adjust so as to be able to make the catch with the ball coming toward him.

What he wants to avoid is chasing the ball, which puts him at the mercy of the wind. That's what causes balls to get dropped.

The best way to make the catch is to hold the glove chest-high, pocket up. If the ball misses the pocket or happens to bounce out of it, you can trap it against your chest.

But most of today's catchers prefer to make the catch with the glove positioned over their heads, just above their faces. And they're successful with it. But when using this method, the catcher loses sight of the ball for an instant just as it enters the glove.

Roy Campanella was well known for his ability to snare pop-ups. He never seemed to miss one. The

Thurman Munson gloves foul fly in accepted fashion.

chance to get his body set to absorb the impact of the impending collision. That's how catchers get hurt.

Of course, the catcher isn't permitted to block the plate until he has possession of the ball. Then he can block it in any way he wants. The runner has similar freedom. He can use any weapon he has

Milt May gives a textbook demonstration on how to block the plate and make the tag. Victim is Lou Brock.

secret of his success, he once said, was that he never watched the ball going up. "All it does is make you dizzy," he said. "There's time enough to watch them when they start coming down. And they always come down. No batter ever left one up there."

Plays at the plate can be extremely perilous for the catcher. While the runner is charging down the baseline, the catcher is usually concerned with trapping the outfielder's throw, and he may not have a

available in attempting to clear the catcher out of the way—his shoulder, knees, or spikes.

Because everything happens so fast, plays at the plate sometimes end in confusion. Colorful Larry McLean used to be a catcher for the Reds and later the Giants. In a game toward the end of his career, a runner tried to score from second on a single to right field. McLean was waiting at the plate with the ball clutched in his right hand. The runner made a desperate slide, raising a cloud of dust.

McLean was sent sprawling and the ball was jarred loose from his grasp. But the runner failed to touch the plate.

Seeing this, McLean scrambled to his feet, recovered the ball, and turned to make the tag. But the dust was so thick, he couldn't distinguish the runner from the umpire. All he could see were four feet, so he tagged each one as fast as he could.

"I don't know which of you is which," he exclaimed, "but one of you is out."

RUNNING THE BALL GAME

Rube Walberg, a star pitcher with the Philadelphia Athletics in the 1930s, once suffered a wild spell on the mound, walking three successive batters. Walberg's catcher, the tempestuous Mickey Cochrane, was seething.

The next hitter stood at the plate with the bat on his shoulder. "Ball one!" the umpire proclaimed as Walberg's pitch plunked into Cochrane's glove. Ball two and ball three quickly followed. Cochrane's face was now the color of a ripe tomato and he glared menacingly out toward his pitcher.

"Ball four!" came the umpire's cry. The batter started for first base and the man on third trotted toward the plate.

Cochrane called time and stormed out to the mound. Without saying a word, he grabbed the startled Walberg by the shoulders, spun him around, and then kicked him right on the seat of his pants. "Settle down!" Cochrane ordered. Then he turned and strode back to the plate.

Walberg seemed shocked at first, but then decided to treat the incident as a joke and forced himself to grin. More important, he settled down, eventually winning the game. Mickey Cochrane should have gotten partial credit for the victory.

Handling pitchers is one of the essential ingredients of becoming a standout catcher (although the tactics used by Mickey Cochrane aren't necessarily recommended). Another is knowing how to handle each individual batter. Together they constitute the art of running the ball game. No other aspect of catching is so important.

A catcher has to be part psychologist and part diplomat in dealing with the many different temperaments represented on the pitching staff. All of the pitchers are likely to respond to praise and encouragement. But some pitchers have to be needled, and the catcher has to know which ones. He has to know which ones can become lazy or careless. In such cases, the catcher will go to the mound and say, "Bear down!" and he must say it like he means it.

"People tend to think of big league pitchers as being pretty much alike," says Dodger catcher Steve Yeager. "They're not; their personalities are very different. It's my job to understand each one. If I know how a pitcher thinks, then I know which way to go with him."

When the Dodgers' Don Sutton is having difficulty on the mound and catcher Steve Yeager spots what's wrong, he hustles right out to tell him. "Maybe he's getting his arm up, or maybe he should slow down," says Yeager. "Whatever it is, he wants to know right now, before the next pitch."

But Yeager can't handle pitcher Andy Messersmith in the same fashion. "If Messersmith is doing something wrong," says Yeager, "he wants me to wait until we're back in the dugout to talk it over. When he's on the mound, he's so competitive that

Pitcher-catcher cooperation is what produces victories. Here Jerry Grote (left) and Jerry Koosman exchange congratulations following a Mets' win.

Terry Humphrey has advice for pitcher Tom Walker.

all he wants to do is throw the ball. He figures if he's doing anything wrong, it will wait."

Sometimes, however, the relationship between the catcher and the pitcher is less than perfect. Carlton Fisk once recalled the problems he had as a rookie in reprimanding pitchers. "How much can a rookie say to a veteran who has been around for a long time?" said Fisk.

"There are times when a pitcher has to be chewed out—given a verbal kick in the butt, you might say. When I was a rookie and tried that, some of the pitchers didn't even hear me."

The short-tempered pitcher is a constant problem for the catcher. When a batter smacks one of his best pitches up against an outfield wall, he can't believe it. He may grouch about it for an inning or two unless the catcher goes out to the mound and calms him down. He'll slap him on the back and say, "Just a lucky hit. That guy must have been praying. Don't let it bother you."

Imagine this situation: It's the eighth inning of a close ball game. There are two men on with two outs. The count is 3 and 2 on the batter. The pitcher rears back and delivers a beautiful breaking ball that just catches the outside corner. The batter, who had been anticipating a curve, stands there and lets it go right by. It's the perfect pitch. How do you think the pitcher feels when the umpire slips up and calls it a ball?

It happens. And when it does happen the catcher usually hustles to the mound, puts his arm on the pitcher's shoulder and says, "Sure, he blew it; he really blew it. But don't worry about it. Don't let it cost us the game. You've got great stuff. Just take your time and throw the pitch I ask for."

Some pitchers always manage to control their emotions, no matter what happens. Bad calls don't upset them, and neither do errors by their teammates. They realize that these things are part of the game.

One of the most even-tempered pitchers of recent times was Whitey Ford of the New York Yankees, recently named to the Hall of Fame. No matter what happened, Ford remained calm. He never sulked. He had enormous confidence in his pitching and his ability to control the situation. He was, according to a Yankee coach, "a catcher's delight."

The first rule in handling a pitcher is to know precisely what he can do—what his best pitches are.

The catcher also has to have an exact mental picture of what the pitcher's motion looks like. When the opposition begins pounding the ball it's sometimes because the pitcher has unconsciously made a change in his motion. Maybe he's increased the length of his stride; maybe he's releasing the ball too soon. Either one of these can cause problems. It's up to the catcher to be able to detect what has happened and tell the pitcher about it.

A catcher's tip can have important value. During

Whitey Ford—"a catcher's delight."

the opening weeks of the 1975 season, the Yankees' Catfish Hunter lost three straight games. The New York management, which had signed Hunter to a $3.7 million contract only a few months before, began to get nervous.

In Hunter's next start, Ed Herrmann, the Yankees' No. 2 catcher, was behind the plate. Herrmann remembered that when Hunter had pitched for the Oakland A's the year before, the Oakland catchers had always kept their gloves very low, about twelve inches off the ground. That's what Herrmann decided to do. Hunter pitched a neat three-hitter, winning easily.

The catcher begins sizing up the pitcher before the game begins, when warming him up. If he finds that one of the man's pitches is not quite up to par, then he'll be wary about calling for it. Suppose the pitcher's curveball is not breaking as sharply as it usually does. Then the catcher may decide to use it only as a waste pitch, to use it when the pitcher is ahead of the batter, that is, when the count is 0 and 2 or 1 and 2. In such cases, the batter won't be getting a good pitch, anyway. It's then that the catcher will merely show the batter the curve, implanting in his mind that it's another weapon the pitcher has available. As the game proceeds, the pitcher's curve may start improving, and the catcher can then start calling for it as a strike pitch.

Sometimes a pitcher will encounter control problems because his timing is off. He'll have good stuff, but he won't seem to be able to get the ball into the strike zone.

Again, the catcher should be able to spot what's wrong. It may be that the pitcher is pushing off from the rubber too soon, and striding forward on his front foot while his arm is still lagging behind. If the pitcher can be told what he's doing wrong, he can probably adjust. "It's easy for me to spot an irregularity in a pitcher's motion," Johnny Bench says, "but it's not so easy for the pitcher. I may tell him to follow through or get his back into the pitch."

Pace is important in pitching, too. Sometimes a pitcher gets so involved with a hitter that he becomes impatient, throwing too quickly. It's up to the catcher to slow things down. He can hold the ball for an extra second or two before returning it to the pitcher, or he can walk out to the mound and hand it to him, telling him to take his time.

Some pitchers don't need coaching help from behind the plate, or very little of it. Luis Tiant, a mainstay of the Red Sox staff for many years, was one such pitcher. "Tiant had been around so long, he always knew what to do," Carlton Fisk once said. "When he made a mistake—and they were rare—he knew it."

The catcher is usually the first one to know when a pitcher is beginning to weaken. The pitcher's fastball may lose its zip, or his curve may start to hang. A hanging curve is one that sits up around the batter's chest, instead of breaking sharply down. The batter can thus tee off on it—and usually does.

What can a catcher do about a pitcher who's hanging curves? Very little. The best policy is to tell the manager to get someone throwing in the bullpen.

Of course, it's the manager who ultimately decides when to make a pitching change. When he comes out to the mound to confer with the pitcher and catcher, he's likely to have his mind made up about what he's going to do. But sometimes he'll get an opinion from the catcher before making a decision, asking him, "Does he still have good stuff?" or "Is he getting tired?" The manager is sure he'll get an honest answer from the catcher. From the pitcher, he's not so sure.

Sometimes it's not easy to analyze what the pitcher is throwing. Take what happened one afternoon many years ago when the Braves were in Boston and scheduled to play the Pittsburgh Pirates. Al Javery went to the mound for the Braves. Phil Masi was behind the plate.

The first Pirate batter hammered Javery's first pitch down the right field line for a triple. The next batter hit the right field wall for a double.

Then in rapid succession the Pirates lashed out a home run, double, single, double, and yet another double—each one on Javery's first pitch.

Manager Casey Stengel, shaking his head in disbelief, waved Javery off the mound and brought in a relief pitcher. Then Stengel called Masi over to the dugout and asked, "What kind of pitch was that guy throwing, anyway?"

"I don't know," Masi answered. "I never got to catch one."

If the catcher had only the pitcher to worry about,

Los Angeles manager Walt Alston, catcher Steve Yeager, and pitcher Doug Rau discuss Rau's status.

the job would not be difficult. But he also has to be able to handle the hitters, outwitting each one in turn.

What this comes down to is knowing the weakness of each hitter, and exploiting it every time the man comes to the plate. It becomes very much of a guessing game, the pitcher and the catcher trying to keep the hitter off balance, and then feeding him the pitch that takes advantage of his weak point.

It's more complicated than it sounds. "When I first came up with the Phillies [in 1973], I didn't have great difficulty with the mechanics of the job," Bob Boone once recalled. "I knew how to handle myself. I had confidence in my arm.

"But getting to know the pitchers and hitters, that was a big problem. How do you get a guy like Pete Rose to hit the pitch you want him to hit? How do you set up Cesar Cedeno for a strike?"

No one expects the catcher to be the sole judge of what the pitcher should throw. He gets plenty of help. Before a series or a game, pitchers, catchers, and the manager and coaches meet and go over the opposition lineup, and the players are given up-to-date scouting reports on each hitter. They learn what batters are hitting the ball well and which ones are slumping. The report tells which batters are having trouble with what pitches. Of course, the pitcher and catcher will also rely on

Carl Yastrzemski—keep the ball outside.

their own store of information on each hitter.

For example, when Red Sox slugger Carl Yastrzemski steps to the plate in Boston's Fenway Park, the catcher, following the "book" on Yastrzemski, is almost certain to call for an outside pitch. The idea is get the left-handed hitting Yastrzemski to hit the ball into right field. The fence in deep right field is 380 feet from home plate. But in left field there's a tall fence only 315 feet from the plate. If you don't keep the ball outside, Yastrzemski is likely to poke it up against the wall in left field for a double.

The book on Tony Oliva of the Minnesota Twins, a marvelous natural hitter, said to feed him pitches inside right on the belt buckle. But what Oliva was likely to do was foul off such pitches, and keep fouling them off until the pitcher missed by a few inches. A base hit—at least—was the result.

Catchers agree that the great Ted Williams, one of the finest natural hitters of all time, had no real weakness. Once he saw a pitcher's fastball and had judged its speed, he could time his swing so as to be able to hit it solidly the next time he saw it. In addition, he could also adjust his swing so as to be able to connect with any other pitch the pitcher might throw. So catchers would not let Williams see their pitcher's fastball until they had two strikes on him and wanted to try for a third.

Most catchers would try to get Williams to hit a low slider breaking down and in. It wasn't, however, a pitch you could call with great confidence. It was just that Williams was less successful in hitting the slider than he was with most others.

The reason for the pregame or preseries meeting is that information about hitters and their likes and dislikes at the plate is subject to change from time to time. Hitters know what their faults are and work to correct them. When Bobby Murcer of the San Francisco Giants came into the major leagues, he liked to chase the high fastball. He would even go for neck-high balls—but never hit them. But in time Murcer learned to discipline himself. Today he waits for the pitcher to miss, to put the ball inside where he likes it.

A hitter can even change over the course of a season, perhaps working with a batting coach to overcome a weakness. A curveball that would have gotten a man out in April, gets slammed for a double in September. So catchers have to keep alert, constantly watchful for changes.

The pregame or preseries meeting may also serve to inform the infielders and outfielders as to how the pitcher and receiver are going to be working on each batter, for this information influences how each player will position himself. For example, if a particular right-handed hitter is going to be fed fastballs on the outside corner of the plate, then the fielders know that there's a good chance he's going to be pulling the ball toward left field, and they adjust their positions in the field accordingly.

Knowing what pitches to throw to what hitters is only the beginning. Calling the right pitch at the right time is an art. "It's something you never really master," says Del Crandall, a splendid catcher for the Braves during the 1950s.

"You want your catcher to stick to your game plan, to pitch to the hitters the way you decided when you went over the lineup before the series or the game," Crandall points out, "but you also expect him to change it in certain situations. It can be confusing.

"You may tell your pitcher that such and such a batter is a low ball hitter, so keep the pitches high and outside. But if the pitcher's best pitch is a low sinker, then he has to call for that anyway.

"The catcher has to know when to use the high fastball just to set the hitter up and when to let him hit it, or *make* him hit it."

Catchers regard each pitch as being either an out pitch or a waste pitch. An out pitch is the pitcher's most effective pitch, the one over which he has the most control and in which he has the most confidence. Nolan Ryan's out pitch is a fastball. With Jerry Koosman of the Mets, it's a curveball.

Some pitchers have more than one out pitch. Tom Seaver of the Mets has three of them—a fastball, curve, and slider. The same with Jim (Catfish)

Catfish Hunter boasts a wide variety of "out" pitches.

Hunter of the Yankees; he's cool and confident with any one of several pitches.

A waste pitch is used to set up the out pitch. It's usually one that the pitcher has not developed fully, and one that he cannot control quite as well as his out pitch.

Control—that's the essential ingredient. "When you have a pitcher that can control all of his pitches, then you have a winner," says Elston Howard, a New York Yankee coach whose skill as a catcher won him ranking as one of the game's all-time greats. "A pitcher may be able to throw every pitch in the book, but unless he can control each one he's not going to be successful."

Control doesn't mean merely the ability to put the ball in the strike zone, described by the rulebook as "that space over home plate which is between the batter's armpits and the top of the knees when he assumes his natural stance." The pitcher has to be able to spot the ball at various points within the strike zone.

The target area that the pitcher shoots for varies with the count. When the count favors the batter, and the pitcher *must* deliver a strike, the target area is relatively large in size. It can be as big as the strike zone itself.

But any time the pitcher gets ahead in the count, thereby diminishing the necessity for still another strike, the target area gets smaller in size. Now it's the pitcher who is in control; the pressure is on the

From behind the plate, the strike zone looks like this. Catcher is Darrell Porter.

batter. He knows he's not going to see a "fat" pitch.

In their duel with the man at the plate, the pitcher and catcher usually follow this strategy:

First pitch: the catcher can call for either an out

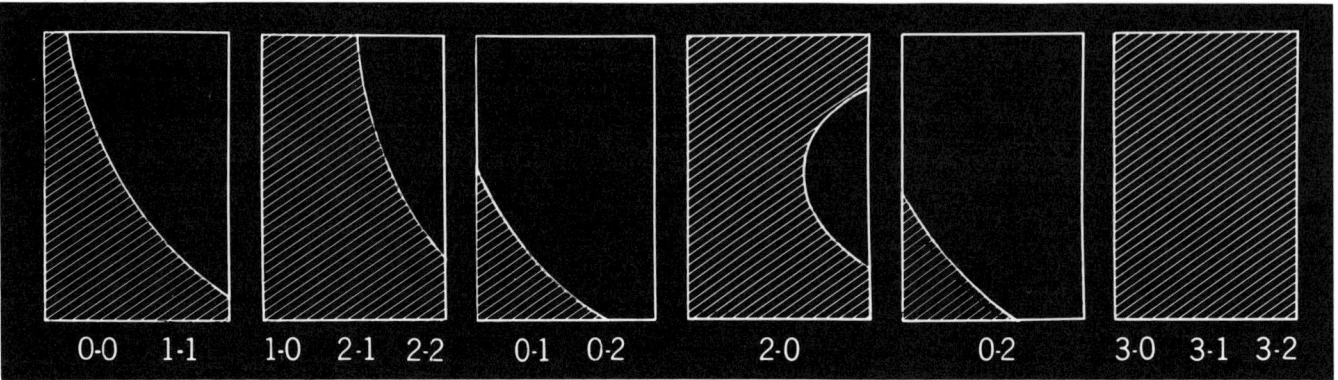

The target area within the strike zone increases or decreases in size, depending upon the count. The more the count favors the pitcher, the smaller the target area becomes. The shaded area indicates how the target area looks to the catcher when there's a right-handed batter at the plate.

pitch or a waste pitch. If the hitter is notably weak, the catcher and pitcher will undoubtedly challenge him with an out pitch. A strong hitter is likely to see a waste pitch, a bad pitch, one used to set him up for the next pitch.

Second pitch: If the first pitch missed the strike zone and the count is 1-0, the pitcher has to come in with a strike. If, however, the count is 0-1, the pitcher is almost certain to deliver a waste pitch, although a weak hitter may see a second out pitch.

Third pitch: If the count is 2-0, the pitcher has to buckle down, coming in with his best out pitch. The hitter is loose and confident, so the pitcher has to work carefully. But when the count is 0-2, it's the pitcher who is in the driver's seat. In 99 cases out of 100, you'll see a waste pitch. The batter knows this, but he still has to be alert, ready to swing at anything that looks close. If the count is 1-1, the catcher can call for either an out pitch or a waste pitch. It depends on the hitter and the game situation.

Fourth pitch: If the count becomes 3-0, the batter's teammates on the bench are likely to be yelling, "You're in charge!" or "He's gotta come to you!" True. The batter is very much in control. The pitcher *must* come in with the ball, perhaps firing right down the middle with all the speed he can muster. The pitcher also needs a strike should the count reach 2-1, but he doesn't need it quite so desperately. While a 2-1 situation calls for an

out pitch, it's a well-controlled pitch. The batter isn't likely to be able to get a good piece of it. If the count is 1-2, the batter is going to see a waste pitch.

Fifth pitch: If the count is 3-1, the pitcher has to throw his best out pitch, coming right down the middle with it. A 2-2 count also demands a strike pitch, but it's not going to be one that the batter has much chance of hitting.

Sixth pitch: When the count is 3-2, you're going to see the pitcher challenge the hitter with an out pitch. He has no other choice.

Throughout the game, the catcher watches carefully to see whether anyone changes his grip or stance. By so doing, the hitter can influence the type of pitch to call. For instance, some hitters, when the pitcher gets two strikes on them, like to shorten up on their grip and edge closer to the plate. By making these adjustments, they feel they're better able to cope with breaking pitches and anything on the outside of the plate. Naturally, the change in stance is going to affect what the catcher asks for.

Catchers watch the batter's feet to see whether the man is looking for a fastball or a curve. Some hitters will move toward the front of the batter's box when they're expecting a curve, hoping to be

Jerry Koosman throws for the inside corner against the Cards' Reggie Smith.

able to swing before it breaks. Others move back when they think a fastball is coming in, the idea being to get as long a look at it as they possibly can.

Some power hitters—the Pirates' Willie Stargell, for one—will overstride in an attempt to pack as much power into their swing as they can. When a catcher sees a batter doing this, he may signal a fastball inside, then follow up with a breaking pitch—a curveball or slider—low and away. When the batter swings, he's almost certain to be off balance.

The catcher asks the pitcher to deliver the pitch he wants through an elaborate signal system. The method of signaling has changed hardly at all in the past century. The theory behind the signals is the same, too. They have to be visible to the pitcher but concealed from the opposition. They have to be simple enough so that the pitcher clearly understands what's being signaled, but confusing enough to deceive the opposition.

The traditional signals are these: one finger for a fastball; two fingers for a curve; three fingers for a change-up or any other type of pitch the pitcher throws—a slider, for instance.

Four fingers are seldom used, but when they are, the fingers are waggled to make the signal more

Traditional signals are one finger for a fastball, two fingers for a curve. A fist is often the signal for a pitchout. Terry Humphrey demonstrates.

When Terry Humphrey wants the pitch to be thrown outside (to a right-handed hitter), this is the signal he gives.

distinctive. Four fingers usually indicate a pitch that's not used frequently, such as a forkball or screwball.

A closed hand, a fist, is the traditional method of calling for a pitchout, a pitch the purpose of which is to make it easier for the catcher to throw to a base. The pitchout is always a fastball. Where it's directed varies. If the catcher's throw is going to go to second and there's a right-handed batter at the plate, the ball should come in high and outside. If the throw is going to third, however, the pitch should be high and tight, backing the batter away from the plate so he won't obstruct the throw.

Suppose there's a suicide squeeze situation, the runner on third streaking for the plate while the batter gets set to bunt. If the man at the plate happens to hit from the left side, the pitchout pitch should be low and outside. Then all the catcher has to do is glove the ball and make the tag. But if he's a right-handed hitter, the pitch should come in high and inside, brushing him back from the plate.

Of course, the signal system can be changed at any time during a game, with one finger used to indicate a curve, two fingers a change-up, and so on.

When flashing the signal, the catcher crouches, then places the heel of his glove near his left knee so that the pocket faces the other knee. He puts his right hand along the inside of his right thigh. By so doing, he conceals the signal from the coaches in the coaching boxes or runners on first and third.

But when there's a runner on second, he's able to see the signal just as clearly as the pitcher, and the system changes. Instead of flashing one finger or two or three, the catcher employs a series of signals. In quick succession, he might flash two fingers, then one finger, then three fingers. The catcher and pitcher have agreed in advance which one of the three is the "real" signal, the meaningful signal.

Sometimes what's called an indicator signal is used to deceive the opposition when there is a runner on second base. Again a series of finger signals is flashed. But the first signal in the sequence merely "indicates" when the real signal is to be flashed. For example, the catcher will flash four signals, the first signal being two fingers. To the pitcher, two fingers means that the signal for the pitch is going to be flashed two signals after the indicator. If the first signal is one finger, it indicates the signal for the pitch is to be the very next signal flashed.

The indicator method of signaling is subject to many variations. For example, the catcher, before flashing any finger signals, may first give an indicator signal by picking up some dirt, or by touching his chest protector or mask. Touching the mask can mean that the first finger signal is the meaningful signal. Picking up dirt can mean that the third finger signal is the real signal.

The catcher can further complicate the system by giving a sequence of signals before the finger signals. He might touch his chest, mask, and right knee in rapid succession. The pitcher knows that when the catcher touches his chest first, that the first of the finger signals that are to follow is the real signal. Or when he touches his right knee first, it means the second finger signal is the real one.

If the catcher or pitcher suspects that the opposition has figured out their signals, has broken their code, so to speak, they make changes. They can make a change between innings, or during an inning, simply by holding a brief conference at the mound.

Sometimes the pitcher looks intently at the catcher as he's giving the signal, then shakes his head or waggles his glove. It appears that he's dissatisfied with the signal and wants the catcher to call something else. This is seldom the case, however. The catcher and the pitcher are almost always in complete harmony in their thinking. When the pitcher looks as if he's shaking off the sign, he's usually simply trying to unsettle the batter, give him something else to think about. It's psychological warfare.

While the catcher gives the signal for every pitch, he doesn't actually order the pitcher what to throw. Most of the time the catcher and the pitcher are thinking the very same thing, and the catcher's signal is simply a confirmation of that thinking.

Of course, the relationship between the pitcher and catcher is subject to countless variations. In the case of a rookie catcher and an experienced pitcher,

His signaling completed, Bob Boone gives the pitcher a target with his glove.

it's the pitcher who's in command. It's very difficult to imagine a young, untried catcher dictating to a Tom Seaver.

In the case of a veteran catcher and a rookie pitcher, the situation is reversed; the catcher will be the boss.

Sometimes the manager calls the pitches, signaling the catcher what he is to signal the pitcher. An inexperienced catcher might get just about all of his signals from the bench. And even a veteran may be under instructions to look to the manager for a signal in any critical situation.

The catcher also signals where he wants the pitch thrown, high or low, inside or outside. He may do this simply by giving the pitcher a target with his glove to throw to, or he may use his bare hand to indicate where he wants the pitch to go. Dodger catcher Steve Yeager points with his thumb to signal whether he wants the pitch inside or outside.

Sometimes a catcher will signal that he wants the ball thrown outside (to a right-handed batter) by touching the inside of his right thigh. Touching the left thigh means that he wants the ball thrown inside.

The palm of the hand is sometimes used to signal high and low pitches. Facing the palm down and waggling the fingers means that the catcher wants a low pitch, low in the strike zone, that is. Facing the palm upward indicates a high pitch.

Once all the signals have been flashed, the catcher gets into his target stance, crouching low, his feet wide apart, his glove positioned exactly where he wants the ball.

When giving the target with his glove, the catcher has to be careful that the batter doesn't turn his head and try to sneak a look. Catchers normally position the glove low for a curve and relatively high for a fastball. If the batter can get a peek at where the glove is, it gives him an idea of what kind of pitch is coming. He also will know whether the ball is going to be inside or outside.

What should the catcher do in such a case? Yankee coach Elston Howard, a major league catcher for fourteen years, gives this advice: "When you have a batter who's turning and looking, then you don't give the pitcher the target until after the guy has turned and looked. Or you just walk to the mound and tell the pitcher where you want the ball."

Or the catcher can even conspire with his pitcher to give a target that's the opposite of where he wants the ball. For example, if he wants a high pitch, he'll squat low and hold the glove low. At the same time, he'll shout out, "Put it right here!" After the batter has taken his peek, the catcher quickly moves the glove into the right position.

It is frequently said that the handling of pitchers is the most important aspect of managing a ball team. No wonder then that so many catchers become managers after their playing days are over. In any

given season, about one-fourth of all major league managers have had playing experience as catchers.

Catchers are often quite successful as managers. Yogi Berra, Ralph Houk, and Mickey Cochrane, all catchers, each won a pennant in his first year as a manager.

Jack McKeon, former manager of the Kansas City Royals, agrees that his experience as a catcher has proven extremely valuable. "The big thing," says McKeon, "is that having been a catcher you're naturally alert all the time.

"A catcher is like a quarterback. He's in on every play. He's not like an outfielder who may handle the ball only three or four times during a game. The catcher has to know what's going on every minute.

"Well, when you become a manager, that attitude carries over. You're constantly 'in' the game. You're always watching, always alert. Being a catcher is the best training you could ask for."

Opposite: **Jack McKeon (left) and Del Crandall (chatting with third baseman Don Money) are among former catchers who managed in the major leagues in recent years.**

STOP, THIEF!

The scene is Busch Stadium in St. Louis, the night of September 10, 1974. The Cards are playing the Phillies.

Lou Brock, the Cardinals' wiry 170-pound left fielder, leads off the seventh inning with a single. The fans cheer loudly. "Lou! Lou! Lou!" they chant as Brock, eyeing pitcher Dick Ruthven carefully, takes a long lead off first base.

Baseball's most successful thief, Lou Brock.

Ruthven throws to the plate. Ron Hunt fouls off the pitch. "Lou! Lou! Lou!" the chant continues.

Ruthven glances toward Brock, then delivers to the plate again. But every eye in the stadium is on Brock. He is streaking toward second, and when he slides in to the base just ahead of catcher Bob Boone's wide throw, pandemonium breaks loose.

Players pour out of both dugouts and photographers stream out into the field. Everyone is clapping Brock on the back and shaking his hand. With this, his 105th stolen base of the season, Brock has broken the modern base-stealing record.

The year 1974 could have been called baseball's "Year of the Thief." Several base-stealing records were set that year.

It wasn't just Lou Brock, who ended the season with 118 steals. More than 1,000 bases were stolen in each league, and that had never happened before. It seemed everyone was running.

The St. Louis Cardinals, as one might expect, led teams in both leagues in stolen bases that season with 172. But several other teams were almost as larcenous. For example, the Oakland A's, well known for their fine hitting and pitching, also ran wild on the bases. A's outfielder Bill North led the American League with 54 steals. Bert Campanaris had 33; Herb Washington, 29; and Reggie Jackson, 25. The team total came to 164, only eight fewer than the Cards' total.

What was the reason for all this thievery? Was

it the fault of the catchers? Had they all suddenly grown weak-armed or sore-armed?

Not at all. As the chart below indicates, catchers in 1974 were about as efficient in throwing out base stealers as they had been in previous years. (The chart begins in 1969, the year the major leagues expanded to twenty-four teams.)

The simple reason that there are more steals nowadays is that many more steals are being attempted. The steal has become an important offensive weapon.

There are many reasons for this. Sparky Anderson, manager of the Cincinnati Reds, blames it on the quality of pitching that is prevalent today, the fact that so many of today's pitchers are able to overwhelm the hitters. "They give you poison," he says. "If you do happen to get a guy on base, you can't wait for two hits or a hit and a long fly. They may never come. You've got to send the guy down."

The sacrifice bunt used to be the accepted method of advancing a runner, and it is still used. But it is not standard procedure any more. Synthetic surfaces

Year	Total Attempts	Stolen Bases	Caught Stealing	Percentage Caught Stealing
		AMERICAN LEAGUE		
1969	1,603	1,033	570	36%
1970	1,415	863	562	40
1971	1,412	865	547	38
1972	1,392	853	539	38
1973	1,719	1,058	661	39
1974	1,992	1,234	758	38
		NATIONAL LEAGUE		
1969	1,365	817	548	40%
1970	1,570	1,054	516	32
1971	1,392	900	492	35
1972	1,520	954	566	37
1973	1,528	976	552	36
1974	1,879	1,254	625	33

have made bunting more difficult. "The sacrifice bunt on artificial turf becomes harder," says Anderson. "The ball rolls so fast and true that the opposition can often get the runner going into second. To get him there, more and more managers are flashing the steal sign.

"Another thing, because of the speed with which the ball slips through the infield and into the outfield, it's much tougher to get a runner from first to third on a single, or from second to home." What's needed today, says Anderson, are "people who can run."

Maury Wills of the Los Angeles Dodgers began the trend toward "people who can run" when, in 1962, he registered 104 steals. (It was Wills' record that Brock broke in 1974.) During the 1970s, several players with the speed and guile equal to that of Wills began to win headlines. There was Dave Lopes of the Dodgers, Joe Morgan of the Reds, Cesar Cedeno of the Astros, Bobby Bonds of the Yankees, and Bill North of the A's.

But most of all there was Lou Brock. The year 1974 was the fourth consecutive year that Brock had led the National League in steals, and the eighth time that he had done so in his career.

Brock stole his 118 bases in 1974 in 151 tries, a .781 percentage. He enjoyed a greater percentage of success against the Cubs than any other team. He made 15 attempts against the Cubs; he was successful 15 times. The Reds—Johnny Bench, that

Bobby Bonds is another of the game's leading base stealers.

is—gave him the most trouble. He made only five attempts against the Reds; he was successful three times.

Brock once said that the "secret" of his success was knowing the opposing pitcher, knowing his best pitch, his release, and his move to first base. According to Maury Wills, "You develop a sixth sense about knowing when the pickoff throw is coming and when it's not. You have a feeling."

The catcher usually isn't the man at fault when a base is stolen. The key element in the successful steal is for the runner to get a long lead and then capitalize on it with an explosive start as the pitcher goes into his windup. Any time the runner fails to get a good jump on the pitcher, the chances are good he'll be thrown out by several steps.

During the 1974 season, when the New York Mets were frequently victimized by base stealers, Manager Yogi Berra was quick to absolve catcher Jerry Grote. "There's nothing wrong with Grote's arm," he said. "He throwing good.

"It's the pitchers. They're not throwing over to first often enough to keep the runners close."

Pitcher Tom Seaver, often a target for the base stealers that season, shouldered some of the blame. "I know that I'm responsible for some of the steals," he said. "I've gotten a little careless. I've been concentrating on the pitches I make rather than on keeping an eye on the base runners."

What does a runner look for when he studies the pitcher? Sometimes it's the pitcher's front knee that tips off where he's going to throw. The pitcher has to bend that knee slightly in order to be able to deliver the ball to the plate.

Runners also watch the way a pitcher turns and leans. Most right-handed pitchers turn slightly toward the base before throwing to it. Or they will lean in the direction of the plate before throwing there.

There are many other factors involved in the steal. For instance, there is a big advantage to the runner if he waits until the count favors the batter. Then the catcher is not nearly as likely to call for a pitchout. In addition, the batter can afford to swing and miss in an effort to make the catcher's throw more difficult.

Certain types of pitches are easier to steal on. A breaking pitch, because it takes longer to reach the plate than a fastball, presents a slight advantage to the runner. A pitch that is low and inside to a right-hander works to the advantage of a runner on first base. There's additional time required on the catcher's part in gloving the ball and making the throw.

A knuckleball is a big plus for a runner getting set to steal. The man behind the plate is likely to have all he can do to catch the ball cleanly, much less worry about making a throw.

Lou Brock, in the year that he set the base-stealing record, was helped a great deal by Ted Sizemore, the man who followed him in the batting

Getting a long lead on the pitcher is the key element in stealing a base. Here Bill Buckner of the Dodgers gets a good jump on the Mets' Tom Seaver, and slides into second base ahead of catcher Jerry Grote's throw. Minutes later Buckner scored on Willie Crawford's single.

order. When Brock was on base, Sizemore would often swing at a bad pitch so as to distract the catcher and thereby give Brock an added split second in his effort to beat the throw. Brock often referred to Sizemore as his "partner in crime."

"Sometimes we'll talk while we're waiting to hit," Sizemore once said, "and Lou will say, 'Give me a strike to check the pitcher's motion.'

"Once he's on base, he might give me a sign to give him another strike."

Sometimes Sizemore would check his swing in order to make the catcher delay his throw by a millesecond or two. "Checking your swing is better than faking a bunt," Sizemore said, "because when the catcher sees the batter shorten up to bunt, he comes out of his crouch and gets ready to throw. But a checked swing keeps him back."

Whether the batter is right-handed or left-handed is also an important matter. A man who hits from the left side is much more of a distraction to the catcher in an attempted steal of second.

Steals of third are usually attempted only when there's a right-handed hitter at the plate. A right-hander partially blocks a catcher's view of third and can also obstruct his throw.

Who the batter happens to be is also a factor. You're not going to see an attempted steal with two outs and the pitcher at bat. Why? Because the runner knows that should he fail, the pitcher will be the first batter to come to the plate in the next

Brock speeds for second.

inning, a situation that isn't recommended to a team trying to generate some runs.

An alert catcher can help prevent steals by studying the base runners and getting tip-offs as to when they're going to be running. A good time for the catcher to check the runner is when he's giving the signal to the pitcher.

The runner may unwittingly reveal that he's going to be trying to steal by tugging at his helmet or hitching up his pants. Or maybe the catcher can flash a look at the third base coach and be able to intercept the steal sign. Then the idea is to throw to first base to try to pick off the runner.

To be able to nail a runner attempting a steal, takes a strong arm, an accurate arm. Catchers have to be almost as concerned about their arms and throwing ability as pitchers do.

Catchers practice throwing every day. Johnny Bench begins by throwing easily, then gradually increases the power and distance of his throws between home plate and second base (a distance of about 127 feet). That's not all. He keeps increasing the distance until he's throwing the ball 200 feet. He's using the same principal that batters use when swinging a weighted bat, he explains. When they step up to the plate, the actual bat feels much lighter than normal. In the same fashion, Bench has no trouble throwing the ball 127 feet when he has to.

Catchers throw directly overhand, snapping the wrist as they release the ball. Whenever possible, they grip the ball so that their fingertips are across the seams, which helps to keep the ball on a straight-line path. It's similar to the way a pitcher grips when firing a fastball.

When throwing to second base, some catchers target on the pitcher, since the pitcher is on a direct line between home plate and second. If the pitcher is off to one side, the catcher is likely to use the pitching rubber in lining up his throw.

Johnny Bench targets on the pitcher's chest. It's up to the pitcher to get out of the way when Johnny unleashes the ball.

Pitchers are not always successful in this regard. When Yogi Berra first joined the Yankees, he was so wild that he once hit a pitcher with a throw to second base. Another time he nailed an umpire.

"Shifting the feet is probably as important as the actual throwing," according to Johnny Bench. How the feet are positioned helps to determine where the ball is going to go. "The best throw in the world won't help you if you miss the base by five feet," says Bench.

The catcher's role in preventing steals keeps getting increasingly difficult. Not only are more and more players inclined to run today, but there's another development—the pinch-running specialist. Herb Washington, a track star who was capable of running 100 yards in 9.2 seconds, was hired on a test basis by the Oakland A's in 1974, not to bat,

Pirates' Manny Sanguillen shows classic throwing form.

field, or throw, but to replace a slower man when he reached base.

Toward the end of the season, Alvin Dark, manager of the A's, said that Washington's speed had helped the team to win at least six games. Washington ended the year with 29 steals in 45 attempts.

The American League, in 1973, introduced the designated hitter who hits for the pitcher. Maybe one day there will be a designated runner, a player with the speed and skill of Herb Washington, who could be used for four or five times in a game without the team being deprived of the services of the man he replaces.

Most fans would be in favor of such a change. It surely would add more excitement to the game.

Catchers feel differently. The designated runner represents a form of excitement they could do without.

In baseball's earliest days, the catcher caught barehanded, and was positioned far in back of the batter. This sketch, from *Leslie's Illustrated Weekly*, dates to 1865.

LOOKING BACK

The Cincinnati Red Stockings of 1869 were baseball's first professional team. From April to mid-November that year, they toured the country from coast to coast, playing all comers. Incredibly, the Red Stockings won 65 games without suffering a single defeat.

The peerless Harry Wright was the team's captain and played the outfield. The pitcher was Asa Brainard, a wily right-hander, praised because he "rarely pitched the ball where the batter expected it."

Doug Allison did the catching for the Red Stockings. It was said of him that a "pluckier catcher could not be found."

Pluck, which the dictionary defines as "courage and daring in the face of difficulties," was a good quality for a catcher to have in those days. Allison, like every catcher, positioned himself ten to twelve feet behind the batter and, bending forward slightly from the waist, caught the pitch on the first bounce.

He wore no equipment, not even a glove.

He kept his feet together to stop low balls. Foul tips would often break through his hands to carom off his chest.

With the catcher positioned far behind home plate, a runner on first could steal second base with ease—and usually did. To prevent this, the catcher would, in a close game, move right up behind home

When the catcher was positioned a good distance behind the plate, stealing second base was a cinch—as this drawing of an "old time base ball game" indicates.

plate. Bruised hands, split lips, broken teeth, and bloody noses were the usual result. But catchers didn't mind, not too much. Injuries and bleeding were a source of pride in those days.

Beginning with baseball's earliest days in the 1840s, the catcher caught the pitched ball on the bounce, moving behind the batter only when the situation demanded that he do so. The latter half of the nineteenth century was a period of experimentation and change for baseball, and one of the most significant developments of this era was the shifting of the catcher to a position right behind the plate. Once that had been accomplished, the modern version of the game can be said to have begun.

The first rules prohibited the pitcher from swinging his hand above the level of his waist when he delivered the ball. In other words, he had to pitch underhand. It wasn't until the late 1870s that the rules were revised to permit overhand pitching.

At one time, the rules also stated that the pitcher had to throw the ball wherever the batter wanted it —shoulder-high, waist-high, or knee-high. This rule was dropped in the early 1880s.

The first rules set the distance between the batter and the pitcher at 45 feet. The distance was increased to 50 feet in 1881, and established at 60 feet, 6 inches—the present distance—in 1893.

There were also equipment changes and innovations during this period, although they came slowly. To wear protective gear of any kind was to risk

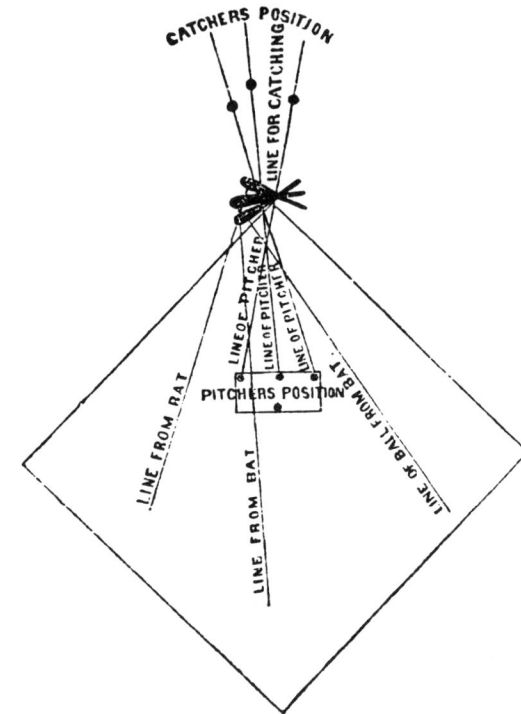

From *The Game of Base Ball*, published in 1868, this diagram shows recommended "stand-points" for the pitcher and catcher.

the ridicule of fans and opposing players. It was not considered manly to protect oneself. Much the same situation prevails in ice hockey today. Most professional players will not wear protective headgear because they consider it sissified.

The first fielders' gloves were similar to the type of glove that batters sometimes wear today, made of thin leather and without any padding. Sometimes the fingers were cut off. The gloves were flesh colored so that spectators would not notice them.

Catchers wore gloves of this type on each hand. Eventually, a little stuffing was added to the glove worn on the left hand.

First gloves for catchers were worn in pairs.

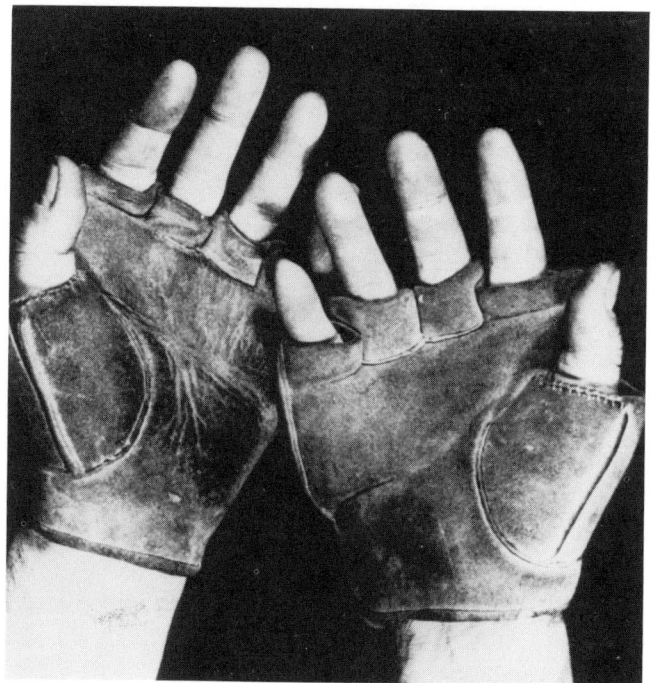

Before the mask was introduced, the catcher sometimes wore a rubber mouthpiece to protect his teeth. The first catcher to hide his face behind a mask was a college player. His name was Fred Tyng and he played for Harvard. Tall, with a handsome profile that he did not want to have rumpled, Tyng wore a fencer's mask to which stiff wire was added. He took a great deal of kidding when he first appeared in it.

Although the equipment that catchers used was primitive by today's standards, the position itself was always regarded as a very important one. Harry Chadwick, a newspaper reported who wrote about baseball as early as 1858, and later was to be the author of several books on the sport, admonished pitchers to "bear in mind that no matter how skillful they may be in the delivery of the ball, they must be largely dependent for success upon the character of the assistance rendered by the catcher."

Catchers were expected to know the weaknesses of the batters, just as they are today. Chadwick said the catcher can "materially aid" the pitcher when he "happens to know the peculiar style of his batting opponent," and then signals him "what kind of ball to send in."

Chadwick expected the catcher to be a leader or, as he expressed it, "Keep a bright outlook over the whole field."

In a book he wrote titled *The Game of Base Ball*, published in 1868, Chadwick had warm praise for

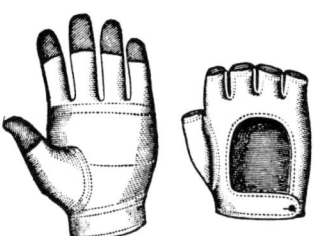

CHEAPEST HOUSE IN AMERICA.

BASEBALL UNIFORMS

$4.00, $5.00, $6.00, $8.00, $10.00, $15.00

Consisting of Cap, Shirt, Belt, Pants, Stockings, Shoes and Plates.

CATCHER'S GLOVES.
From 25c. to $4.50 per pair.

CATCHER'S MASK.
$1.50, $1.75, $3.00, $3.50.

UNIFORM BAGS.
Made of Heavy Canvas,
Leather Bound, $1.00 each.

STEEL SHOE PLATES.
10c., 25c. and 50c. per pair.

H. H. KIFFE, Brooklyn, N. Y.
SEND FOR CATALOGUE AND SAMPLES.

Not until the late 1800s were catchers wearing masks along with gloves.

several catchers of the day. He singled out Kelley of the New York Actives for his "pluck and coolness," and Radcliffe of the Athletics for "facing the swift music courageously." Another player, Buckley of Irvington, was also praised "for his courage in bearing punishment from swift pitching."

During the 1880s, baseball became a more exciting game. Pitchers learned how to curve the ball, and sliding developed into an art form, with players diving headfirst or feet first, or hooking the base with a hand or a toe as they slid by. The first league—the National League—was founded in 1876. The American League didn't come into existence until 1900.

By way of comparison, there was no pro football in 1876, and it was to be another fifteen years before Dr. James Naismith was to invent basketball. People skated, but only a handful of Canadians had ever heard of ice hockey.

Several catchers achieved national renown during the 1880s. Jim O'Rourke, who took part in the first National League game ever played—Boston vs. Philadelphia on April 22, 1876—was the first. Besides catching, O'Rourke sometimes played the outfield, third base, or first base. Line drives sizzled from his bat and he had a powerful arm. He was once credited with a throw of 365 feet.

A major leaguer for twenty-three years, O'Rourke was known as "Orator Jim" because he had a large vocabulary and loved to talk. His trademark was an elegant mustache.

Hall of Famer Jim O'Rourke was known for his slashing hits and flowing mustache.

O'Rourke was a member of the Boston team in 1878 when the management tried to make players pay for their own uniforms. Rebelling at this idea, O'Rourke successfully "jumped" to the Providence team. This act led to the creation of baseball's "reserve rule," later to be adopted by owners of teams in pro football and other sports.

Michael Joseph (King) Kelly was another early catching star. During the 1880s, when the Chicago White Sox were the scourge of baseball, Kelly was the most popular player of the day. "There was hardly a boy in the land," says Lee Allen in his book, *Kings of the Diamond*, "who did not follow the daily doings of 'the King.'"

Kelly was an innovative player, and some sources say it was he who invented the hook slide. The phrase, "Slide, Kelly, slide," which was part of the language for more than half a century, was first applied to him. Kelly always said that he was the first catcher to use finger signals in telling the pitcher what to throw. Maybe he was: nobody knows for sure.

Besides being an innovator, Kelly was also something of a schemer. He used to drop his mask in the basepath or on home plate in an effort to discourage the runner from coming in too fast. The rules now prohibit this.

In Kelly's day, the rulebook said that a substitution could be made at any time. One day Kelly was sitting on the bench, when a foul fly was hit toward him. Kelly jumped up and shouted out, "Kelly now catching," whereupon he settled under the ball and made the catch. That winter the substitution rule was changed.

Bill Holbert (left) and A. J. (Doc) Bushong were among baseball's earliest catchers. Holbert, who played for the New York Metropolitans, was described as "earnest, quiet, faithful, and an effective worker." Bushong, who caught for Worcester, accompanied the team on a trip to Havana in 1879.

A major league player for sixteen seasons, Kelly left a lifetime batting average of .313.

William (Buck) Ewing has been called "the greatest catcher of the 19th century." A gentle, good-natured man, always a favorite of the fans, Buck began his career in organized baseball with the Rochester team of the old National Association, then moved on to the Troy Haymakers. When the Haymakers disbanded, Buck signed with the New York Giants. The $3,200 he received in 1882 was, acording to *The New York Times*, the "highest salary ever paid a ball player." In his first year with the team, Buck led the National League with ten home runs.

Many sources credit Ewing with being the first catcher to throw the ball to second base from a

crouch. "It wastes time to straighten up," he used to say. It was many years, however, before other catchers saw the advantage of Ewing's style and began using it.

Ewing benefited from a sunny personality. He was always warm and smiling in his dealings with the umpires. "You called that one just right," he would say. "It *was* outside." The umpire would feel pleased, and if there was any doubt on the ensuing call, it was likely to be made in Ewing's favor.

Jim O'Rourke and Mike Kelly were elected to baseball's Hall of Fame in 1945. Buck Ewing was elected in 1946.

Even in Ewing's time, catchers were still wearing two gloves, although the amount of padding in each had been increased. Still, the pitcher could not fire the ball with his utmost speed, being limited by the courage (or recklessness) of the catcher. "It was impossible," said one catcher of the time, "to do anything but get the ball and hang on."

It wasn't until the final decade of the nineteenth century that the art of catching began to resemble more closely what it is today. In 1891, the A. G. Spalding Company received a patent for a catcher's mitt, circular in shape, pillow-like in appearance.

The mitt made for enormous changes in the game.

Buck Ewing is rated as the very best of the early catchers.

THE SPALDING PERFECTION CATCHERS' MITT

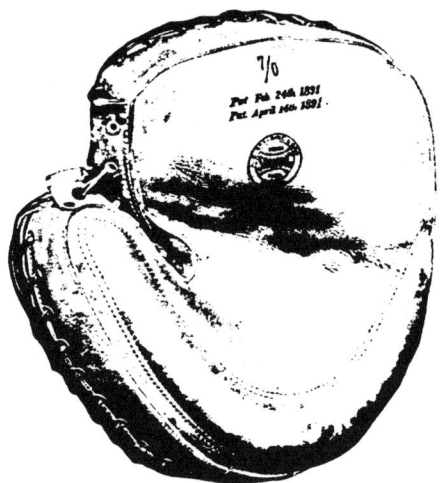

FOR years our No. 7-0 Mitt has been considered as near perfection as it was possible to come in making an article of this kind. The leather is of finest quality calfskin, padding of best felt hair obtainable, and every other detail of manufacture has been carefully considered, including patent lace back with rawhide lacing. Thumb is reinforced and laced, double row of stitching on heel pad and strap-and-buckle fastening at back.

No. 7-0 $6.00

A. G. SPALDING & BROS.

New York, Chicago, Philadelphia, San Francisco
St. Louis, Boston, Buffalo, Baltimore
Denver, Minneapolis, Kansas City, Montreal, Can.
London, England

The "big mitt" enabled the catcher to move up close behind the plate.

SPALDING CATCHERS' MITTS

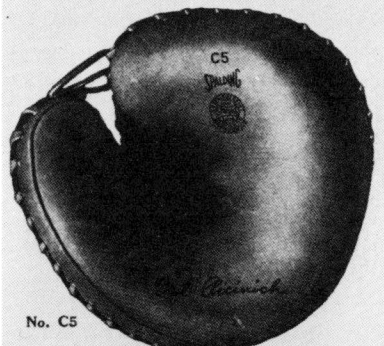

No. 9-O / No. 9-O Back View

Al Lopez

No. 9-O. Professional model. A molded mitt of golden brown horsehide. Hand-formed padding. Felt padded wrist strap. Very popular with semi-pro and college teams. . . . . Each, $8.00

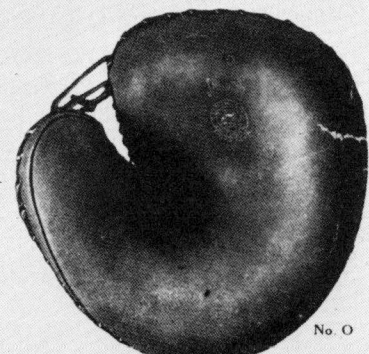

No. C5 / No. O

Val Picinich **No. C5.** Specially selected golden brown grain horsehide leather; patented one-piece molded face; leather bound throughout; adjustable lacing at thumb; special hand-formed padding. This mitt is the same size as our No. 9-O mitt and is very popular with colleges and semi-pro teams throughout the country. . . . . . Each, $6.00

★**No. O.** Special tan shade horsehide leather; semi molded face; adjustable lacing at thumb. It has a large pocket and needs very little breaking in. A very popular mitt with junior, prep and high school teams. Same size as our No. C5. . . . . . Each, $5.00

★ *Also carried in stock in full right for left hand players.*

PAGE 14—JANUARY 5, 1932

Left: **By the 1930s, mitts had changed little.**

"The introduction of the new mitt is the thing that made the catcher one of the most important men on the team," said John (Rowdy Jack) O'Connor, whose comments appear in a booklet, "How to Play Baseball," published in 1903. O'Connor was a leading authority on the subject. He had begun his catching career in the finger-glove days of 1887 with the Cincinnati Reds, and twenty years later he was still at it, having played for seven different teams in that period.

"With the big mitt behind the bat," said O'Connor, "the scientific game had to be invented. Bunting, place hitting, and the hit-and-run game were the chief features of the scientific game," O'Connor maintained.

What the big mitt did was permit the catcher to move up behind the plate where he could keep an eye on the base runners, and do something about it when one of them tried to steal. As O'Connor put it, "It became unsafe to steal." Now, he said, "the catcher could pay attention to the game."

The big mitt was one of several equipment advances that date to this period. Obviously, players' attitudes toward protecting themselves were changing.

The chest protector made its debut in 1884, with Jack Clements of the Pittsburgh Keystones the first to wear one. By the early 1900s, the chest pro-

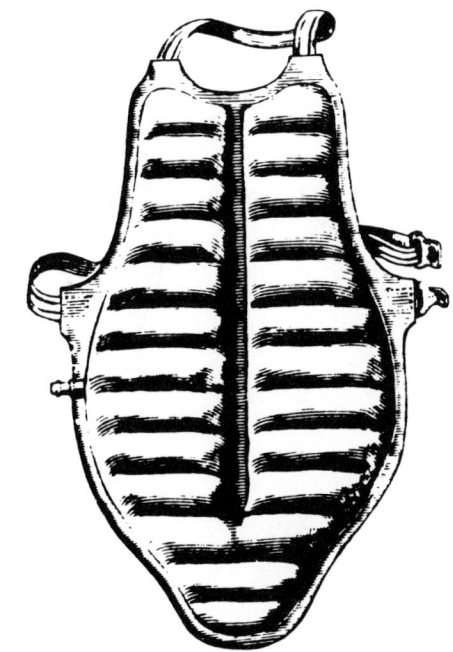

The A. G. Spalding Company offered this "inflated body protector" in 1903.

tector was similar in size and shape to the one in use today, but instead of being padded with foam rubber, cotton batting, or some similar material, it was filled with air. You blew it up in the same way you inflate a toy balloon.

Shinguards were first used by Red Dooin of the Phillies, but Dooin wore them furtively, trying to conceal them by wearing them under his stockings.

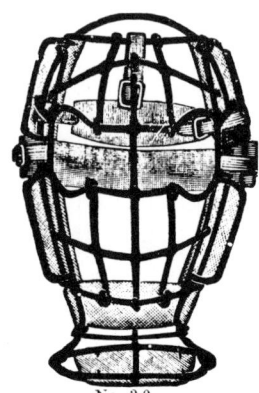
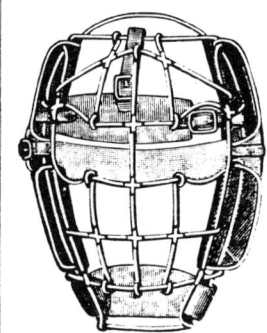

Some masks of the 1890s protected the neck as well as the face.

Roger Bresnahan pioneered in the use of shinguards.

The first catcher to wear shinguards openly was Roger Bresnahan who won stardom with the New York Giants in the early 1900s. Bresnahan purchased a pair of white shinguards meant for use in the game of cricket, and wore them for the first time in a game at New York's Polo Grounds in 1907. You'd have thought that he was wearing a ball gown. Jeers and catcalls poured from the stands when he emerged from the dugout. Opposing players hooted at him throughout the game.

"Boy, they sure called me lots of names when I first put them on," Bresnahan was to recall in later years. "But I guess they were a good idea; catchers are still wearing them."

Bresnahan was elected to the Hall of Fame in 1945, but not simply because of his spunk. He was considered the outstanding catcher of his time, and when Christy Mathewson pitched three shutouts in the 1905 World Series, it was Bresnahan who was behind the plate. He was unusually fast for a

Gene Tenace wears a helmet of shell plastic, most recent equipment development for catchers.

catcher, and often batted as the Giants' leadoff man.

Bresnahan was also one of the first players to experiment with a batting helmet. Always a plate crowder, he was once hit in the head by a steaming fastball and seriously injured. When he returned to the game, he wore a padded helmet. It was not until 1958, fourteen years after Bresnahan's death, that batting helmets became mandatory in major league

Bresnahan would surely have applauded the newest piece of protective equipment that catchers wear, the shell-plastic catcher's helmet. It's similar to the batter's helmet, except that it's visorless.

Once the catcher was fitted out with protective equipment, and no longer had to be quite so concerned about getting hit or injured, he could devote more attention to the game's strategy. An instruction booklet for young players written in 1905 and titled *How To Catch* declared that "the catcher's most important business is to fool the batter." That was revolutionary. Previously, he was mostly worried about catching the ball, or at least stopping it. The era of modern baseball had dawned.

THE BEST

When professional baseball was celebrating its first one hundred years in 1969, fans, sportscasters, and sportswriters were asked to select the greatest players ever, by position. When the ballots for catchers were tabulated, three names headed the list—Mickey Cochrane, Roy Campanella, and Bill Dickey.

Two others whose names were close to the leaders were Yogi Berra and Gabby Hartnett. What about Johnny Bench? At the time the balloting was conducted, Bench was a second-year man with the Reds, yet to undergo the test of time.

"The best catcher I ever saw was Mickey Cochrane," Arnold Hano once wrote in *Sport* Magazine. He described Cochrane in these terms: ". . . a thick shag of black hair . . . glittering black eyes . . . a sweat-slick beard of black bristles." You always heard him on the field, said Hano, no matter where you sat. "You could almost feel him."

A splendid hitter, extremely fast and smart, Cochrane made his first major league appearance in 1925 for the Philadelphia Athletics, remained in the team's lineup for nine years, and then was sold to Detroit. While with the Tigers, he was the victim of a tragic accident that put an end to his playing career.

Mickey Cochrane

Cochrane caught 100 or more games for eleven successive seasons. He left a batting average of .320 for his thirteen-year career. His best average for a season was .357, attained in 1930.

But Cochrane is best remembered for the way in which he inspired his teammates. He would snarl at them, branding them as "yellow-livered buzzards" or the like, if he thought they were performing at anything less than their best. He simply could not stand to lose.

Cochrane was a minor league player with the Portland Beavers of the Pacific Coast League when he came to the attention of the Philadelphia team, then managed by the fabled Connie Mack. But the asking price for Cochrane was much more than Mack was willing to pay. He had a solution, however. He simply bought controlling interest in the Portland team, thereby obtaining Cochrane's contract.

Years later, Mack was to say: "It's not often that you buy a whole club to get one player, but I've never regretted that purchase. I'd gladly buy another club to get another Mickey Cochrane."

Cochrane's fiery leadership, his day-to-day excellence behind the plate, and his dependable bat helped to propel the Athletics to pennants in 1929, 1930, and 1931. He was named the American League's Most Valuable Player in 1928 and then again in 1934.

The A's trounced the Cubs in the 1929 World Series and did the same thing to the Cardinals in 1930, but against the Cards again in 1931, the A's ran into trouble, trouble by the name of Pepper Martin. A rookie that year, the brash Martin, much to Cochrane's dismay, stole five bases. The Cards won the series in seven games.

It was later revealed that Martin's success on the basepaths stemmed in part from the antics of Jimmie Wilson, the St. Louis catcher, and the man who batted behind Martin. Whenever Martin reached base—and he batted .500 for the series—Wilson did whatever he could to harass poor Cochrane, blocking his vision and sometimes poking his bat at Cochrane's glove. Cochrane became so jittery he even dropped a third strike.

Wilson, incidentally, was a first-class catcher. Unlike Cochrane, however, he was a quiet and reserved person. He also caught for the Reds and Phils and later managed. His lifetime batting average of .284 puts Wilson in Yogi Berra's class as a hitter.

Cochrane was sold to Detroit in 1933 for more than $100,000. He became the Tigers' manager and steered the team to its first championship in twenty-five years in 1934. He won another pennant, plus the World Series, the following year. It was Cochrane himself who scored the winning run in the sixth and final game, when he singled in the bottom of the ninth inning, advanced to second on an infield out, and scored as Goose Goslin lined the

Roy Campanella

ball into right center. When Cochrane reached home plate, he jumped on it again and again and again in his enthusiasm.

Early in the season of 1937, the Tigers faced the Yankees. Cochrane came to bat with a runner on first base. Bump Hadley was the Yankee pitcher.

In an effort to pull the ball behind the runner, Cochrane was crowding the plate. The count went to 3 and 1. When Hadley's next pitch sailed up and in, Cochrane lost sight of it momentarily and it struck him with a sickening sound just above the right eyebrow.

Cochrane dropped in front of the plate, his skull fractured in three places. He was unconscious for most of the week that followed.

When he was released from the hospital, Cochrane wanted to go back behind the plate. But the Detroit owner, Walter O. Briggs, acting on the advice of medical experts, would not permit him to do so. Thus ended Cochrane's playing career. He was released as the Tigers' manager in 1938. He died in 1962.

Easy-going, soft-talking Roy Campanella had a personality that was quite the opposite of Cochrane's, yet he earned a reputation as one of baseball's greatest catchers in a ten-year career with the Brooklyn Dodgers that began in 1948. He excelled in steadying pitchers and gunning down base runners, and his powerful bat was an important reason why the Dodgers won pennants in 1949, 1952, 1953, 1955, and 1956. Campy captured the National League's Most Valuable Player award three times—in 1951, 1953, and 1955.

A "nice guy" was the way Campanella was usually described. But his teammates and opposing players knew him to be a shrewd man, a leader. "Campy was the brains," said Monte Irvin, an outfielder with the New York Giants during the early 1950s. "We didn't fear anyone on the Dodgers as much as we did Campy."

It was Campy's bat that was feared the most. One day against a Cincinnati pitcher named Ken Raffensberger, Campanella hit three consecutive home runs, each time with a man on base. When Campy came to the plate the fourth time, Raffensberger was still on the mound. He stared in toward the plate as Roy swung his bat menacingly. "You aren't going to hit one this time," Raffensberger shouted. And he promptly walked Campy on four straight pitches.

Campanella established a major league record for the most home runs in a season by a catcher when he hit 41 homers in 1953. (The record now belongs to Johnny Bench; Bench hit 45 home runs in 1970.) For his career, Campanella amassed 242 homers, a total second only to Yogi Berra's, and Berra played nine more years than Campy.

Campanella was masterful in handling the Dodger pitchers, a staff that included a number of wild-armed young fireballers. He coaxed some remarkable performances from such pitchers as Ralph Branca, Rex Barney, and Don Newcombe. "When they get in trouble, they right away want to start working faster," Campanella once said. "They snatch that ball when I throw it back to them. They can't wait to fire the next pitch.

"That's when I start picking up a little dirt around the plate to slow things down. I wait a while before I throw the ball back. Or I'll go out to the mound and talk to the guy."

Campanella was twenty-seven years old when he joined the Dodgers as a regular in mid-1948. He had been playing organized baseball since the age of thirteen, beginning as a catcher for the Nicetown Athletic Club in Philadelphia, where he was born. Campy was always big for his age, and an umpire once stopped a game in which he was playing because he thought the burly youngster behind the plate was sixteen. Actually, Roy was then only fourteen.

This being several years before baseball's racial barriers were to come down, Roy, at sixteen, signed with a team in the Negro leagues. He barnstormed the country, appearing in as many as 150 games a season. There were days when he would catch a doubleheader in the afternoon, catch a night game later, and then board the team bus for the long ride to the next stop. He once caught both games of an afternoon doubleheader in Cincinnati, and that night caught a second doubleheader in nearby Middletown. "I wasn't tired," he recalls. "I was young and I didn't mind."

Campanella was playing for a Negro All-Star team in Newark, New Jersey, in 1945 when the Brooklyn Dodgers contacted him, and he signed with the club the following year. He was sent to a minor league team in Nashua, New Hampshire, managed by Walter Alston, later to be the Dodger manager. A season at Montreal in the International League followed, and then Roy joined the Dodgers.

Campanella's career was tragically shortened. Very early one January morning in 1958, he was driving to his home on Long Island, when his car hit a patch of ice and began to slide. After slamming into a telephone pole, the car went into a spin and turned over.

Campanella's neck was broken and his spinal cord severed. He was left paralyzed in both arms and legs.

"After the accident, I knew I wasn't a ball player any more," he once said. "It was over.

"Some people fight themselves about what could have been. I never did. I knew I had to learn to accept the wheelchair—and I did."

Today Campy is active in the operation of his

Campanella makes frequent appearances at events such as this "Old Timers' Day" celebration.

liquor store in New York's Harlem. He lives in Westchester County and he makes frequent public appearances, and is invariably greeted with a standing ovation.

Ask Campanella himself to name the greatest catcher of all time, and Josh Gibson is the name he gives you. "I couldn't carry Josh's glove," Campanella says. "Anything I could do, he could do better."

You won't find Gibson's name on anyone's all-time All-Star team, nor does it appear in any major league record book. Gibson played in the Negro National League.

Some people say that Gibson may have been the hardest hitter in all of baseball history. A good-sized man—6-feet-2, 230 pounds—with thick arms and legs, Gibson is credited with almost 800 home runs in his seventeen-year career. "I never saw any other power hitter like him," Campanella once said. "Most home run hitters strike out a lot, but not this guy. He didn't strike out 25 times in a season."

The Negro teams of the 1930s and 1940s played as many as three games a day and 175 to 200 games each summer. The opposition was furnished by other Negro teams, or semipro teams, such as the Brooklyn Bushwicks, who sent many players into major league baseball.

Many of Gibson's home runs have become legendary. Gibson and Babe Ruth were the first players to punch the ball into the trees beyond the center field fence at the old Griffith Stadium in Washington. In several seasons, Gibson hit more home runs at Griffith Stadium than all the sluggers in the American League combined. He is said to have hit the only fair ball to go over the roof of Yankee Stadium. It landed in the left field bullpen. Gibson was often billed as the "Babe Ruth of the Negro Leagues" or the "Brown Bambino."

While he is remembered as a hitter first, Gibson was no slouch as a catcher. "At first, he was terrible," Ted Page, a one-time teammate of Gibson, told the Washington *Post* not long ago. "He couldn't catch a *sack* of baseballs. We called him 'Boxer' because he'd catch like he was wearing a boxing glove.

"But he worked hard learning. He even caught batting practice to sharpen his skills."

In time, Gibson learned how to handle every pitch thrown, and in the Negro leagues "every pitch" meant an unusual assortment—spitters, screwballs, mud balls, and "shine balls." The shine ball carried Vaseline—so much, recalls one player, that "it made you blink your eyes in the sun."

Observers agree that Gibson had a fine arm, that he was quick and accurate. But another of his teammates, James (Cool Papa) Bell, has said that Campanella was a better defensive catcher than Gibson. "Josh didn't have sure hands like Campanella," Bell said. "But he was smart, smart, and fast.

"Sometimes he dropped the ball on purpose to get some guy to run. And he threw a light ball. You could catch it without a glove. Campanella threw a brick."

Gibson died at the age of thirty-six in 1947, just three months before Jackie Robinson became the

Bill Dickey

first Negro to don a major league uniform.

Most catchers of the 1920s and 1930s were solidly built and stocky. "Squat" was the word often used to describe them. But that term could never be applied to Bill Dickey of the New York Yankees. Tall and lean, Dickey looked as if he'd be much more at home on a basketball court than sitting on his heels behind the batter.

He looked like a natural any time he stepped up to the plate, however. He batted .324 in 1929, his first full year with the Yanks and, except for the 1935 season, he never finished below .300 until very late in his career. He did not hit for distance at the beginning, preferring to line the ball to center field or right center, but little by little he developed into a home run hitter. One year—1937—he had 29 home runs, and he ended his career with a total of 202.

It may have been the company he kept. As a rookie in 1928, Dickey could number Babe Ruth and Lou Gehrig as his teammates, and later he and Gehrig became close friends and they roomed together when the team traveled.

Although Dickey was not fast on his feet, his ability to anticipate plays enabled him to pounce on bunted balls like a cat. His size, at first regarded as a handicap, eventually became an asset. Passed balls were a rarity anytime Dickey was behind the plate. One year he had none at all. His arm was quick and strong.

Dickey was one of the first catchers to discard the pillow-size mitt of the day in favor of a lighter weight, much slimmer model, a mitt more like the one that first basemen used. It enabled him to spear inside and outside pitches with greater facility.

In his seventeen-year career with the Yankees, Dickey caught four Hall of Fame pitchers—Herb Pennock, Waite Hoyt, Red Ruffing, and Lefty Gomez. Ruffing and Gomez were said to be his favorites, even though the latter caused him some anxious moments.

One day the unpredictable Gomez threw a curve after Dickey had signaled for a fastball. Dickey stormed to the mound. "What are you doing?" he fumed. "That's a good way to get me killed."

"How are your bird dogs, Bill?" Gomez asked, pretending not to hear.

Dickey later explained how he managed to cope with the free-spirited Gomez. "I just quit giving him signs," said Dickey. "I'd set myself for a fastball, figuring I could adjust to the curve is he happened to throw it. That was a lot safer than being set for the curve and having that high hard one of his smash into my mask."

Dickey was the American League's All-Star catcher six times and he appeared in eight World Series. In the 1932 World Series, his first, he batted .438. The Yankees swept the Cubs in four games. Against the same team in the 1938 Series, Dickey batted .400. He had a total of five home runs in World Series play.

It's not his heroics at the plate that stand out in Dickey's memory, however. "Don't forget," he once told an interviewer, "that I stole a base in a World Series game." Indeed, he did—in 1932.

What was Dickey's greatest moment in baseball? It occurred, not during his playing days, but later, in 1949, when he was a coach for the Yankees. The team didn't win the pennant that year until the final day of the season, then began the World Series with a tense pitching duel between the Yankees' Allie Reynolds and Don Newcombe of the Brooklyn Dodgers. Tommy Heinrich opened the ninth inning with a home run to win the game for the Yankees. "I don't think while playing," Dickey once said, "that I ever got quite the thrill that I got from that World Series game."

One other of Dickey's accomplishments must be mentioned. As manager of the Yankees in 1946, Dickey worked diligently to improve the catching techniques of a twenty-one-year-old prospect named Yogi Berra. Ironically, it was Berra who was to eclipse many of the Yankee records that Dickey had set.

It would take several pages to list all of Berra's records. These are among his most noteworthy: He was the first player to hit a pinch-hit home run in the World Series. He did it in 1947. He caught in the most Series (14) and in the most Series games (75). He led the league four times in fewest errors. He leads all catchers in home runs with 358, only three fewer than outfielder Joe DiMaggio, one of the Yankees' all-time greats.

Yogi Berra

Three times he was named the American League's Most Valuable Player—in 1951, 1954, and 1955.

Had Yogi not been offended by the St. Louis Cardinals at an early age, he might have won all those awards and set all those records in the National League. He and his boyhood chum, Joe Garagiola, later to become a noted sportscaster, were both standout junior players in their native St. Louis. Garagiola was a catcher; Berra, a third baseman. Both won tryouts with the Cardinals. Garagiola impressed the Cards, and they offered him $500 to sign. Berra was impressive, too, but less so. He was offered only $250. "No dice," said Berra. "You have to give me as much as you gave Joey." The Cards refused.

Berra went back to playing amateur baseball, eventually to be signed by the Yankees, who did feel he was worth a $500 investment. After a year of minor league baseball, Berra went into the Navy for two years. He joined a Yankee farm team in Newark, New Jersey, following his discharge.

Toward the end of the 1946 season, the Yankees brought Berra up from Newark to appraise his talents. He hit a home run in his first major league game and got another the next day. For the seven games in which he played, Berra hit .364, and the Yankees began thinking that the $500 was money well spent.

In spring training with the team the next year, Berra was frequently a disappointment as a catcher.

Baseball's Greatest Catchers

	Games	AB	H	HR	RBI	BA	PO	A	E	FA	HOF*
Yogi Berra	1696	7555	2150	358	1430	.285	9194	919	125	.988	1972
Roy Campanella	1183	4205	1161	242	856	.276	6520	550	85	.988	1969
Mickey Cochrane	1451	5169	1652	119	832	.320	6409	840	111	.985	1947
Bill Dickey	1712	6300	1969	202	1209	.313	7866	954	108	.988	1954
Gabby Hartnett	1790	6432	1912	236	1179	.297	7562	1269	143	.984	1955
Elston Howard	1138	5363	1471	167	762	.274	6447	479	51	.993	——
Ernie Lombardi	1542	5855	1792	190	990	.306	5694	845	143	.979	——
Al Lopez	1918	5916	1547	52	652	.261	6644	1116	123	.984	——
Ray Schalk	1726	5306	1345	12	594	.253	7155	1810	175	.981	1955
Jimmie Wilson	1525	4778	1358	32	621	.284	4916	931	136	.977	——

* Year elected to Hall of Fame.

His fingers were so short and stubby that pitchers had trouble reading his signs. When he threw the ball toward a base, no one was ever sure where it was going to go. The Yankees began experimenting with him as an outfielder. But because he could hit with power and hit consistently, no one thought about sending him back to Newark.

Little by little he began improving as a catcher, especially when the Yankees brought back Bill Dickey to work with him. Dickey showed Berra how to shift his weight and balance so as to be able to control his powerful throws. He helped in his handling of pitchers and showed him how to run a ball game.

Once Berra had mastered the skills, he came to rank, along with Roy Campanella of the Dodgers, as the outstanding catcher of the time. He had a remarkable memory which enabled him to recall minute pieces of intelligence about each hitter. Pitchers rarely shook him off.

Though short and thickset—5-feet-8, 190 pounds—Berra was extremely agile. Two spectacular plays that he pulled off in the opening game of the 1953 World Series are evidence of that. The Yankees faced the Dodgers. With the score tied, 5-5, in the seventh inning, Brooklyn had runners on first and second with none out. Billy Cox bunted toward third base. Berra ripped off his mask, sprang for the ball, and rifled it to Gil McDougald at third, forcing Gil Hodges.

The next batter, Clem Labine, also bunted. Berra went through a replay, leaping out to get the ball and firing it to McDougald to force the runner. In the Yankees 9-5 win, Berra also contributed a home run and a single.

Berra was almost always devastating at the plate in World Series play. As a rookie player in the 1947 Series, Berra slammed a pinch-hit home run, the first ever in Series competion. He hit .429 in the 1953 Series, and .417 in 1955. The following year he personally destroyed the Dodgers' Don Newcombe, who had won 27 games and the Cy Young Award. Berra belted a grand-slam home run off Big Newk in the second game, and unloaded two more home runs in the seventh game, won by the Yankees, 9-0.

The 1956 Series was highlighted by Don Larsen's perfect game. When the twenty-seventh consecutive batter went down, Berra broke from his position behind the plate to leap jubilantly into Larsen's arms.

Baseball writers often portrayed Berra as a dim-witted figure, one who subjected himself to ridicule every time he opened his mouth. He was never as dumb as he was painted. He was always colorful, however, and he did produce many more laughs than the average player.

When with the Newark Bears in 1946, the year before he joined the Yankees, Berra read comic books avidly. "I like the ones about crooks best," he said. He happened to be rooming with Bobby Brown, later to be the Yankees' third baseman, who was studying to be a doctor. As they turned out the lights one night and Berra put aside his comic book, and Brown a thick medical textbook, Yogi asked, "How did your book come out, Bobby?"

When asked what he liked best about school, Berra would reply, "Closed." What was his favorite subject? "Recess."

Once, Berra was at the plate and the pitcher worked the count to 0-2. The next pitch was high and on the outside. Berra could scarcely have reached it with a stepladder, yet he swung—and missed. He threw the bat aside and stalked back to the dugout. Nobody said a word. Berra finally broke the silence by blurting out, "How can a guy that wild stay in the league?"

After he retired as a player, Berra enjoyed a successful career as a manager, leading the Yanks into the World Series in 1964. After the club failed to rehire him, he signed with the New York Mets as a coach. As the Mets' manager in 1973, he steered the team to the National League pennant, only to lose to the Oakland A's in the World Series.

Berra was later successful as manager of the Yanks and Mets.

Many catchers, like Berra, go on to careers as managers. The man who succeeded Berra as the Yankees' catcher, and later became a coach for the team, is often mentioned when managerial candidates are being pondered. His name is Elston Howard.

From St. Louis, Howard, who joined the Yanks in 1955, continued the Yankee tradition of catching excellence established by Bill Dickey. Howard set the American League record for putouts (939) in 1964, a year that he committed only two errors in 150 games. His fielding average of .998 that season marked the third consecutive year he ranked as the league's best fielding catcher. Howard was the American League's Most Valuable Player in 1963.

After being traded to the Red Sox in August, 1967, Howard played a vital role in Boston's successful pennant drive, steadying the young Boston pitchers and contributing with his bat. Young Jim Lonborg, who won 22 games that season and captured the Cy Young award, credited Howard for much of his success. "Ellie takes charge out there," said Lonborg. "He worries about the base runners, how the infielders and outfielders are positioned, and all the other things. All I have to do when he's behind the plate is concentrate on pitching. He makes it easy for you."

Bill Dickey was once asked to name "the perfect catcher." His choice was Charles Leo Hartnett.

Elston Howard

Hartnett earned the nickname "Gabby" because he wasn't. On a long and often lonely train ride across the continent to the California training camp of the Chicago Cubs in 1922, Hartnett, a twenty-one-year-old rookie at the time, hardly uttered a word. Calling him "Gabby" never failed to get a laugh.

As the years went by, however, the nickname became appropriate. A big man for his day—6-feet-1, 215 pounds—Hartnett would stride to his position behind the plate, his chest puffed out confidently, wearing an engaging smile, greeting opponents and nodding to the fans. He looked like a politician touring a favorite neighborhood. Once the game began, he talked incessantly, and frequently he'd shake his fist in the air to inspire his teammates. When an opponent struck out, Gabby would hold the ball aloft in triumph, and then pepper it around the infield while chortling gleefully—conduct that might have earned him the nickname "hotdog" today.

Gabby—most of his teammates called him Leo—had a powerful throwing arm and he loved to use it. There may never have been another catcher as dependable as he was in grabbing foul flies. New York sportswriter Jimmy Powers once noted that Hartnett had missed only three foul flies in some 1,790 games behind the plate.

Hartnett caught 100 or more games per season for twelve years, eight of them consecutively, a

Gabby Hartnett

league record. He batted .300 or better in six different seasons, and was the first catcher in major league history to hit more than 200 home runs. He was the National League's Most Valuable Player in 1935.

Hartnett was behind the plate in the 1932 World Series, the Cubs against the Yankees, when Babe Ruth is said by many to have pointed to the Wrigley Field bleachers, and then put a home run there. But according to Hartnett's version of the incident, Ruth was merely reacting to some boisterous comments from the Chicago dugout. With two strikes on him, Ruth held up one finger to indicate that it only takes one swing to hit it. His towering drive happened to land where many people thought he had pointed.

Hartnett himself once hit a homer that has become almost as notable. The year was 1938. Hartnett, in the final stages of his career, was then managing the Cubs at the time. At the tail end of the season, the league-leading Pirates came into Wrigley Field for a crucial three games with the second-place Cubs.

Chicago won the first game of the series to move within one game of the Pirates. The second game, a long affair, was tied at 5-5 at the end of eight innings. It had gotten so dark that the umpires huddled at home plate to consider whether to continue. They decided to try to make nine full innings.

The Pirates went down quickly in their half of the ninth. Hartnett came to bat with two outs. Mace

Ray Schalk

Brown, a curveball specialist, was on the mound for Pittsburgh.

Although the gathering darkness made a fastball the logical choice, Brown fed Hartnett a breaking pitch. The burly catcher swung and missed. The huge crowd groaned.

Another curve came breaking in. Hartnett swung and fouled it back.

Brown pitched again. Still another curve. Hartnett, squinting to see, swung and sent the ball soaring over the left field wall. Before Hartnett had reached second base, spectators by the hundreds had poured from the stands. A picture in a Chicago newspaper the next day showed a stream of fans and ushers trailing Hartnett around the bases.

The 6-5 victory put the Cubs in first place and two days later they wrapped up the pennant. Hartnett always said his "home run in the dark" was the high point of his career.

Following his career as a player, Hartnett managed the Cubs for two seasons. His last season in baseball was 1965, a year he served as coach for the Kansas City A's. Hartnett died in 1972.

There's one other Hall of Fame catcher who must be mentioned—Ray Schalk of the Chicago White Sox. Although not a big fellow—5-feet-7, 155 pounds—Schalk was extremely durable, and caught 100 or more games in 12 seasons, 11 of them in succession, beginning in 1913.

Schalk owns several catching records. He compiled the largest total of assists (1,810) and led the American League in putouts more times (9) than any other catcher. Alert to move to any part of the field to back up a play or cover a base, he stands as the only catcher in the game to have made putouts at every base—first, second, third, and home.

Schalk was a more valuable hitter than his .253 lifetime average might indicate, for he was very dependable in critical situations. In 1920, hitting only .270, he drove in 61 runs; in 1922, he drove in 60 runs while batting .281.

Durability is a word that has been used frequently in this book. The all-time leader in that department has to be Al Lopez. In his long career that began with Brooklyn in 1928 and ended with Cleveland in 1947, Lopez caught 1,918 games, the record.

He was also rated as one of the game's smartest catchers. This quality was apparent in the years that he managed. His winning percentage of .721 (111 victories, only 53 defeats) as manager of the Cleveland Indians in 1954 is the American League record.

Al Lopez is a logical candidate for membership in the Hall of Fame. Ernie Lombardi, who was mentioned in an earlier chapter, is certainly another. When the Reds won the National League pennant in 1939 and 1940, Lombardi was the key man.

Al Lopez

It's as a hitter that Lombardi is first remembered. Line drives sizzled from his bat, causing shortstops to play so deep that their throws barely

when he faced Lombardi, feared that he'd get injured by drives off the big man's bat.

The reason that Lombardi never won election to the Hall of Fame may have had to do with his image. During his playing days, he was frequently regarded as a clownish figure. His bulbous nose won him the nickname "Schnozz." His pants drooped. While he could hit and throw, he could not run. There's a story that he hit a ball all the way to the fence at Cincinnati's old Crosley Field, but still got thrown out at first base. Lombardi said the story wasn't true. "Lumbering" was the word often used to describe him. Lombardi could never deny that he lumbered.

No book that speaks of baseball's most noted catchers would be complete without some mention of Mickey Owen, catcher for the Brooklyn Dodgers during the early 1940s. Owen will always be remembered, but not for inspiring his teammates, hitting timely home runs, or anything like that; Owen committed catching's outstanding "goof."

It happened in the 1941 World Series, with the Dodgers facing the New York Yankees. The heavy-hitting Yanks won two of the first three games, but in the fourth game the Dodgers went into the ninth inning leading, 4-3, and appeared to be on their way to squaring the series at two games apiece.

With two out and nobody on base, Tommy Heinrich came to bat for the Yankees, and he worked

Ernie Lombardi

reached first base without bouncing. Pitcher Carl Hubbell of the Giants feared for his personal safety

the count to 3 and 2. Pitcher Hugh Casey went into his windup and fed Heinrich a sharp breaking curve. Heinrich swung and missed.

But what should have been the game's last out became a costly misplay. The ball got by Owen, and Heinrich made it to first base easily.

Joe DiMaggio followed with a single to left field, and then Charlie Keller doubled in Heinrich and DiMaggio. The Dodger fans sat in stony silence.

Bill Dickey walked and Joe Gordon doubled in two more Yankee runs. The Dodgers lost 7-4.

Baseball historians have always had a fondness for immortalizing the game's "goats." On any such list, Owen's name is right at the top or very close.

In Bench's big hands, the bat looks tiny.

SUPERCATCHER

Talk about the game's great catchers and you begin with "Orator Jim" O'Rourke, with his slingshot arm and powerful bat, and the popular Buck Ewing, the first catcher to snap off throws to second base from a crouch. There was Roger Bresnahan, always a scrapper, who had the audacity to wear shinguards *openly*.

Later came "Black Mike" Cochrane, who played the game with the intensity of a street brawler. There was the colorful Gabby Hartnett, whose "home run in the dark" helped win a pennant for the Cubs. There was the brilliant Bill Dickey, the Yankees' receiver during many of their glory years.

In the 1950s there was Yogi Berra, and then his successor, Elston Howard. There was the ill-fated Roy Campanella.

Today there's Johnny Lee Bench. The experts say he may outdo them all.

People first began to hear about Johnny Bench early in 1966. Dave Bristol, a coach for the Cincinnati Reds, was one of the first to herald the coming of the 6-foot-1, 200-pound muscle man.

Bristol had just finished managing a Cincinnati team in the Florida Instructional League when he happened to meet a Cincinnati newspaper reporter. "Wait until you see this kid catcher the Reds have," said Bristol. "Name's Johnny Bench.

"He's a winning type ball player. He's smart,

strong, and what an arm! Wait until you see him. You won't believe he's real."

Bench had played briefly with Tampa in 1965, then moved on to the Peninsula team in the Carolina League. Although Johnny played in only 98 games there, he performed with such distinction that the club retired his uniform. Promoted to Buffalo in the International League, he did even better, and was named "Minor League Player of the Year" by *The Sporting News*.

Bench didn't start out as a catcher, but as a pitcher. As a high school player in Binger, Oklahoma—population, 603—he won 16 out of 17 decisions, batting .675 at the same time. He also played occasionally at first base and third base.

"But everybody knew that I was going to be a catcher," Bench says today. His father, who had taken note of the fact that the major leagues had a serious catcher shortage at the time, laid out a training program for his young son. He taught Johnny not merely to throw to second base, but to aim at a particular target—the second baseman's belt buckle, his knee, or a particular corner of the base. And instead of teaching Johnny to throw the distance from home to second base, which is slightly more than 127 feet, he taught him to throw *twice* the distance, about 250 feet. When it came to catching in games, throwing 127 feet was a cinch.

Bench was everybody's star of the future when he joined the Reds in 1968, and he wasted no time in living up to his promise. With 15 home runs, 82 RBIs, and a .275 batting average, he captured Rookie of the Year honors.

His throws to the bases, which traveled like bullets, were the envy of every other catcher in the league. The speed of Bench's throws sometimes handcuffed Cincinnati infielders. "You see the ball coming so low," said Red shortstop Woody Woodward, "and you're sure you're going to have to one-hop it. But it keeps right on coming, never more than two feet off the ground. Then it explodes on you."

Once, early in his career, the Reds were playing the Los Angeles Dodgers. Maury Wills was on first base for the Dodgers. After getting his usual good jump, Wills broke for second. Bench caught the pitch, reached into his mitt, but the ball stuck there. He fished it out on his second try—and still nabbed Wills at second.

In grabbing the ball and throwing it, Bench is aided by big hands and long fingers. He can hold as many as seven baseballs at a time in his right hand.

Just as important as what he did behind the plate or as a batsman, were the leadership qualities Bench displayed. Even as a rookie, he never hesitated about calling pitches. His teammates called him "The Little General," for his willingness to give orders.

Pitcher Jim Maloney, a seven-year veteran with the Reds when Bench arrived upon the scene, once said, "I'm about ten years older than Johnny, yet

On throws to second, Bench is deadly.

he'll come out to the mound and chew me out as if I were a two-year-old. So help me. It's so bad that the coaches kid me about it."

Bench was not the perfect catcher when he arrived in the major leagues. Low pitches were a problem. During his rookie season, he was charged with 18 passed balls and he had 14 in his second year. He was thus averaging a passed ball about once every ten games.

One a month is more his average now. He began improving in the handling of low pitches when he realized why he was having difficulty. When he would warm up a pitcher during training, he never donned his protective gear—his shinguards, chest protector, or face mask. No catcher does. He just grabs his mitt, squats down, and starts catching. If a warm-up pitch happens to go into the dirt or hit the plate, the catcher may make a halfhearted attempt to get the ball, but what he's more likely to do is duck out of the way. Bench realized he had developed some bad habits as a result of warming up pitchers.

So he made it a habit of never catching a warm-up unless he wore all of his protective gear. When a low pitch came in, he trained himself to glove it. In other words, a warm-up session for a pitcher became a practice session for him.

Bench also showed consistent improvement as a hitter. In 1969, he hit 26 homers and upped his batting average to .293. In 1970, at the age of twenty-two, Bench hit 45 home runs, drove home 148 runs, and again batted .293. He was the National League's Most Valuable Player that year.

Bench rates high in popularity polls.

Bench's big arms are rock hard.

As for the Reds, they ran away from the other teams in their division, but then fell meekly in five games to the Baltimore Orioles in the World Series. Everything Bench hit in the series seemed to wind up in Brooks Robinson's glove at third base.

Bench could now look back on three years as a major league player, three glittering years. Then came 1971. The base hits stopped falling in and the home runs no longer boomed from his bat so frequently. He was to see his batting average fall to .238 and his home run production drop to 27.

The previous year sportswriters had begun referring to the Cincinnati team as "The Big Red Machine," scarlet being the color in which their uniforms were trimmed, machinelike being the way they ground out one victory after another. The always hustling Pete Rose, slugging Tony Perez, and swift Bobby Tolan helped to make the machine hum. But Bench was the vital cog. When Johnny was going well, the machine played a happy tune. But in 1971, when Bench slumped, the machine developed a noticeable clank. By August of that year, the Reds were trailing the leaders by 15 games.

Bench, the one-time darling of the fans, was booed often that year, a new experience for him. "I don't think anyone ever got more boos in one year than I got," Bench said after the season was over. "You try to say to yourself, 'Well, the fans pay to get in, so they've got a right to boo!' You say that and you hope you don't hear them. Well, I heard them. I heard them and it hurt."

How did Bench react? When the season was over he went to the Florida Instructional League and spent ten days trying to overcome some bad hitting habits he had developed. He trimmed his weight from 215 to 202 during the off season. In the early workouts the following spring, he acted like a rookie battling for a job. He worked on his batting, caught batting practice, and played the outfield and first base. "I had to find out," he said, "which Johnny Bench was the real Johnny Bench—the one in 1970 or the one in 1971."

He was determined to do well in 1972, perhaps too determined. He had only one hit in his first 22 at-bats, and boos rolled from the stands once more. But before April was over, Johnny's bat had warmed up. In one streak in June that season, he banged out

Bench handles catcher's glove as if it were a first baseman's mitt.

seven home runs in five games. The booing stopped, of course.

Back on the winning track, the Reds captured the National League's Eastern Division title, then faced the Pirates in the playoffs. Bench has a reputation for delivering key hits. None was ever more timely than that enormous home run he struck in the final playoff game against Pittsburgh. What rendered the blow "very great," as sports columnist Larry Merchant termed it, was the fact that Bench "was up there to hit one."

The Reds were behind, 3-2. Ace Pittsburgh reliever Dave Giusti was on the mound.

Giusti worked the count to 1-2. In such a situation, most hitters try to protect the plate, edging closer, shortening up on their grip. Not Bench. "I just knew I was going to hit it," Bench was to say in a postgame interview. "I took a full swing.

"When I touched home plate and looked over and saw the guys coming out of the dugout toward me, it was the greatest sight in the world. Their faces were so excited and they were smiling from ear to ear. I really think it was the greatest moment of my life." The Reds went on to win the game, 4-3, and by virtue of the victory, the pennant.

In the World Series that year, the Oakland A's furnished the opposition. Bench's memories of what happened are not pleasant ones.

The games were hard fought, with five out of the first six being decided by one run. The night before

Although not a speedster, Bench is considered a good base runner. *Right:* Bench cocks his bat as pitch approaches.

the seventh game, Bench and Oakland's superoutfielder, Reggie Jackson, had dinner together. Jackson had suffered a leg injury during the playoffs, and was on crutches. During the meal, Johnny predicted a critical situation would develop the following day, and he would come to bat to face Oakland reliever Rollie Fingers. "He's gotten me a couple of times," Bench told Jackson, "and now it's my turn."

What happened made Johnny seem psychic. In the eighth inning, the Reds trailing, 3-1, Pete Rose opened with a single up the middle. Joe Morgan belted a double into right field, Rose holding at third.

Into the game came Rollie Fingers. Pinch-hitter Joe Hague popped to the shortstop for the first out.

Bench was the next batter. As he tossed aside one of the bats he had been swinging and strode toward the plate, he looked over toward the Oakland dugout. Reggie Jackson was grinning at him and shaking his head. Johnny knew that Reggie was thinking about what he had said.

But that wasn't the only reason that Jackson was grinning. He knew that Oakland manager Dick Williams had ordered Bench to be purposely passed. With Fingers' first pitch, Bench knew it, too.

Tony Perez got the Reds a run with a long fly to right field. Minutes later, Denis Menke popped up to end the inning. The Reds went down without rallying in the ninth, and Bench was on the defeated side once more.

Bench and teammate Pete Rose.

"My job is to drive in runs."

The walk to Bench raised a couple of questions. It violated one of the game's axioms, which is: Never intentionally put the winning run on base.

But that's exactly what Dick Williams had done. Asked about it, all Williams would say is, "I wasn't going to let Bench beat me with his bat."

A reporter then asked Williams if he could remember ordering the potential winning run to be walked ever before. Williams said he couldn't.

In mid-December following the World Series, Bench underwent chest surgery to remove a benign lesion from one lung. Though weakened that season, he still managed to hit 25 home runs and drive in 104 runs. The Reds won their division title for the second consecutive year, but fell victim to the New York Mets' sharp pitching in the playoffs.

The Reds let the Dodgers get off to a big lead in 1974, and were never able to catch them. Bench, back in top form, led the league in RBIs with 129. He had 33 home runs.

In terms of batting average, Johnny's best years have been 1969 and 1970, when he hit .293. He hit .280 in 1974. The fact that he has never topped .300 has caused some criticism, however mild.

Cincinnati manager Sparky Anderson is quick to answer the critics. "If Johnny wanted to," says Anderson, "he could concentrate on hitting for a higher average. But he's a power hitter, a free swinger. And he's not always patient with the bat."

Besides catching, Bench has also played third base (above), first base, and the outfield.

Bench manicures plate between batters.

Bench has this to say on the subject: "My job is to drive in runs and that's what I'm always trying to do."

Bench has proven extremely durable. Even so, he plays a number of games each year at other positions—at first base, third, and in the outfield. "It helps you at the plate," he says. "When I'm in the outfield, I get more of a chance to think about what the pitchers are throwing and about what I should look for when I'm up there batting. Catching absorbs all of your attention."

Bench passed something of a milestone in 1974 when he played in his 1,000th major league game. He could look back on a long list of achievements, including two Most Valuable Player awards (in 1970 and 1972) and seven Golden Glove awards as the National League's best fielding catcher. In addition, he had never failed to be a member of the League's All-Star team since his rookie year.

Before his much-publicized marriage in 1975, Bench was one of the most desirable bachelors in sports. He was good looking, articulate, intelligent, wealthy, and a devoted son. (He moved his entire family, including his parents, a brother and a sister, to Cincinnati to join him.) But while he was known to date and take an occasional drink, he never had a reputation as a swinger. "Cincinnati is a quiet city," he once said, "as American as apple pie. People there expect me to have a wholesome image."

But it was more than that. Bench realized that he ranked high on most lists that judged the popularity of athletes among young people. He had a sense of commitment about this, about living up to certain standards of conduct. He always felt that he owed his fans something more than his best efforts on the field.

The season of 1975 was an unforgettable one for Bench and his Cincinnati teammates. They piled up a club record of 108 victories, claiming the title at the earliest date ever in the history of divisional play. Johnny's .283 batting average was his highest since 1970. He also contributed 28 home runs and 110 RBIs.

The Reds swept three games in a row from the Pirates in the playoffs to capture their third National League pennant in six years. The Red Sox were the playoff winners in the American League.

The World Series was one of the most exciting and dramatic in years. It was deadlocked after six games and eight innings of the seventh game. But in the ninth inning, Joe Morgan looped a single into center field to score Ken Griffey with the deciding run.

The next day there was a joyous celebration in Cincinnati, with thousands of people jamming downtown streets to welcome the Reds. "We're No. 1! We're No. 1!" the crowd chanted.

Now that Johnny's right hand sports one of those big diamond rings that world champions wear, he has only one other ambition. "I want to be the greatest catcher ever to play this game," he says. The chances are good that he will be.

YOU'RE THE CATCHER

Every World Series seems to produce its heroes and goats. The 1917 World Series, in which the Chicago White Sox defeated the New York Giants, was no exception.

The White Sox had the outstanding hero—pitcher Urban Faber, who beat the Giants three times. The Giants had the goat—in fact, they had several of them.

In the fourth inning of the sixth and what was to be the deciding game, Eddie Collins, perhaps the fastest base runner of the day, came to bat for the White Sox. Neither team had been able to score. Collins slammed a grounder to Henry (Heinie) Zimmerman, the Giants' third baseman. When Zimmerman made a throwing error, Collins scampered all the way to third.

The next batter, Oscar (Happy) Felsch, hit the ball right back to the pitcher, John (Rube) Benton. Not trusting himself to make the throw, Benton dashed toward the third base line, the ball cocked behind his ear, chasing Collins back to the base. At the last instant, he threw to Zimmerman in an attempt to get Collins at the base.

But Collins was too quick, and abruptly reversed direction. Zimmerman quickly fired to catcher Bill Rariden who was guarding the plate.

Back to third went Collins, Rariden pursuing him. As Collins neared the base, Rariden threw the ball to Zimmerman.

The elusive Collins instantly broke for the plate, Zimmerman chasing him. The huge crowd at New York's Polo Grounds was on its feet and screaming.

Collins ran right by Rariden who was standing in the basepath. Zimmerman was right at Collins' heels, his arm upraised, ready to throw the ball. Suddenly a look of horror crossed Zimmerman's face. There was no one to throw to; the plate had been left unguarded.

Collins turned on the speed and easily outsprinted Zimmerman. When he crossed the plate, he wore a wide grin. The other White Sox players "hopped around like jumping jacks" in their glee, said a newspaper account of the game.

While Collins was being chased up and down the line, the other White Sox runners advanced to third and second. Minutes later they both scored on a resounding double off the wall. The White Sox now had three runs, one more than they would eventually need. The final score was 4-2.

The next day the press lashed out at Zimmerman, calling his desperate chase of Collins "one of the stupidest plays ever seen in the World Series." But the criticism was unjust. Zimmerman was not the real goat.

What had happened to Rube Benton, the Giants' pitcher? Why hadn't he been in on the play?

And what about catcher Bill Rariden? One of the axioms of catching is "Never leave the plate unguarded when there is a run in scoring position." It's a rule that's as basic to the position as wearing shinguards. Rariden, in violating the rule, not only cost his team a run, but perhaps the ball game and even the World Series as well.

You can talk about the importance of handling pitchers and the ability to gun the ball to second base on attempted steals, but catching is also a thinking man's position. Several times during a game, the catcher is likely to be faced with a critical choice, and the game's outcome may hang on his decision.

The pages that follow enable you to test your ability as a tactician. As the catcher, how would you react in each one of the situations described? (The answers are to be found at the end of the chapter.)

1. The St. Louis Cardinals are playing at Philadelphia. It is the top half of the fourth inning, one out, the score tied, 1-1. Lou Brock is on third base for the Cards, Reggie Smith on first. As Steve Carlton goes into his windup, Smith takes off for second base. Brock dances off third. What should catcher Bob Boone do?

(A) Hold the ball and block the plate, waiting for Brock to arrive.

(B) Throw to third base, the idea being to trap Brock off third and thereby involve him in a rundown.

(C) Look down the line toward Brock, freezing him; then throw to second base to get Smith.

2. The Dodgers are playing the Mets at Shea Stadium. Tom Seaver is pitching for the Mets and he has been sharp, striking out five batters in the first four innings. The game is scoreless as the Mets come to bat in the bottom of the fourth. Leadoff man Dave Kingman triples. Joe Torre is the next batter.

If you were catcher Steve Yeager, you would:

(A) Wave the infield in, the idea being to hold Kingman at third in the event Torre hits a ground ball.

(B) Wave the infield back, conceding the run to the Mets should Torre hit a grounder. The strategy here is to protect against a big inning.

(C) Walk Torre intentionally, and then have the infield play back to try for a double play.

3. The New York Yankees and California Angels are locked in a tight pitching duel at Anaheim Stadium. With none out in the bottom of the seventh inning, the Angels have runners on first and second. Left-handed hitter Mickey Rivers is the batter. In moves the Yankee infield, expecting a sacri-

fice. Rivers obliges, bunting the ball toward third base. Thurman Munson whips off his mask, waves away third baseman Graig Nettles, and barehands the ball. Where does Munson throw?

(A) To first base.
(B) To second base.
(C) To third base.

4. The Boston Red Sox and Baltimore Orioles, playing at Memorial Stadium, are tied at the end of nine innings. Carl Yastrzemski opens the tenth inning with a double off relief pitcher Grant Jackson, then moves to third on Bernie Carbo's infield out. As designated hitter Cecil Cooper comes to the plate, Baltimore manager Earl Weaver waves his infield in to hold Yastrzemski at third base. On Jackson's first pitch, Cooper drills a ground ball to shortstop Mark Belanger. Yastrzemski breaks for the plate. Belanger throws to catcher Andy Etchebarren. What should Etchebarren do?

(A) Drive Yastrzemski back to third, then throw to the third baseman.
(B) Drive Yastrzemski back to third, then throw to first to nab Cooper.
(C) Hold the ball and block the plate to Yastrzemski.

5. The Oakland A's, trailing the Kansas City Royals by a run, are batting in the bottom of the ninth inning. There are no outs. Reggie Jackson draws a base on balls, then races to third base on Joe Rudi's single. Gene Tenace lifts a foul pop-up to the third base side of home plate. Only catcher Fran Healy has a chance of catching it. As Healy pursues the ball, he knows that the runners are going to be tagging up, hoping to advance. Should Healy:

(A) Make the catch and then throw to the pitcher covering home plate?
(B) Make the catch and then throw to second base?
(C) Let the ball drop, which precludes any advance?

ANSWERS

1. The basic objective here is to get an out at second while not permitting Brock to score; (C) is the best alternative. Boone's quick glance toward Brock will cause him to hold up, and there will still be time to fire to second base to get Reggie Smith, Smith not being noted for his speed.

Boone then has to stay alert, guarding the plate and awaiting a possible return throw. If Smith should become involved in a rundown between first and second, Brock is almost certain to break for the plate.

There is one other alternative in this situation—a decoy throw. Instead of freezing Brock, Boone can attempt to lure him toward the plate by not

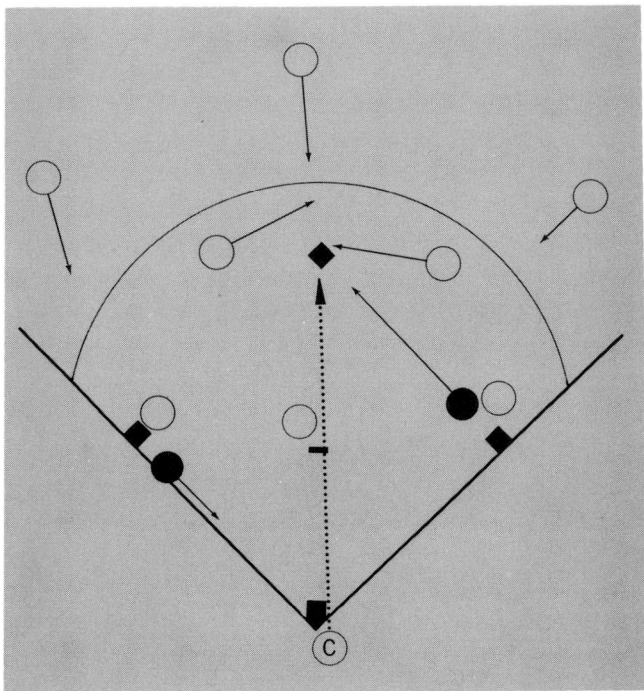

2. When Tom Seaver is going well in a close game, it's never wise to concede him anything. Yeager is almost certain to pull the infield in (A), and try to make Torre hit the ball on the ground. If the Dodgers manage to retire Torre without Kingman scoring, Yeager may then signal to have the next man intentionally passed so as to set up a double play.

bothering to look in his direction. Boone then throws, not to second base, but to the pitcher, and the pitcher fires the ball right back, hopefully to nail Brock as he comes sliding in.

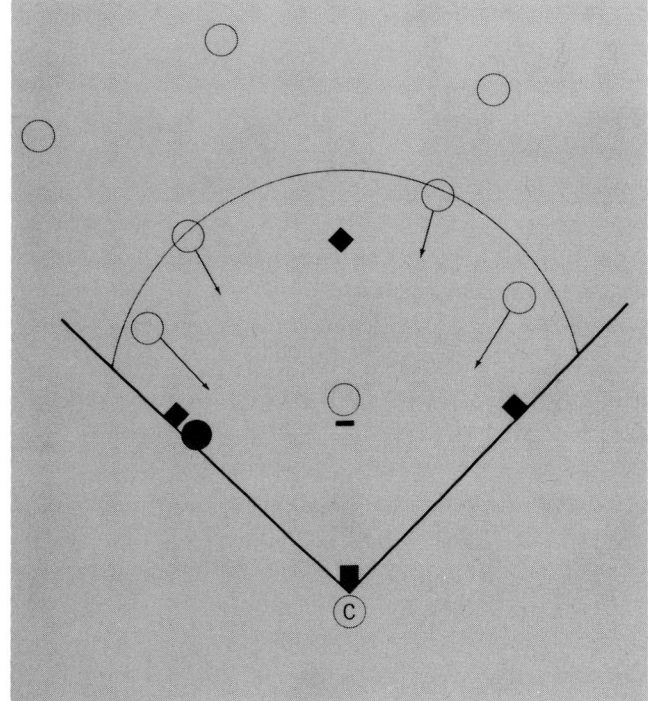

3. While Munson would like to get the lead runner coming in to third base, he realizes that there's not going to be anyone there to throw to, at least momentarily. Nettles' assignment is to cover against the bunt, while shortstop Jim Mason, occupied with keeping the runner close to second base, is delayed in getting there. Second base, too, is going to be unguarded, since second baseman Sandy Alomar must cover first base. First baseman Chris Chambliss is covering against the bunt in the area between first base and the mound. Munson has no choice but to throw to Alomar at first base (A); it's his only sure out.

4. Etchebarren's objective is to nail Yastrzemski, and do it as quickly as possible, before Cooper has a chance to get to second base. Were Etchebarren

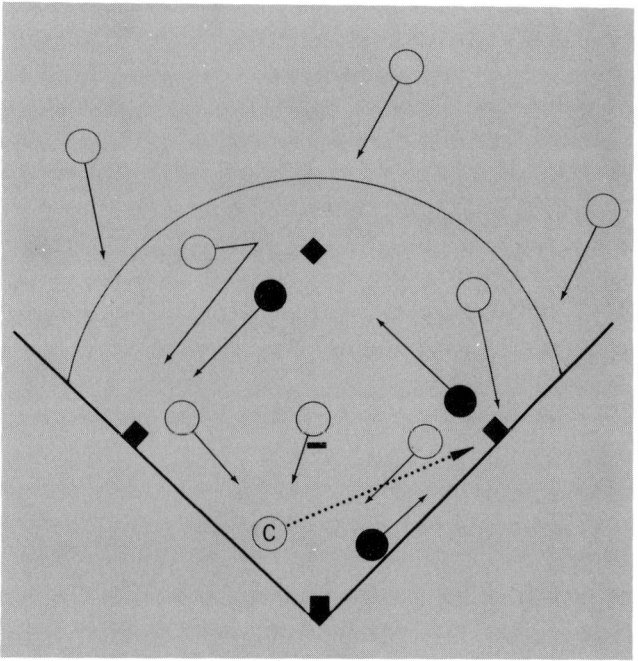

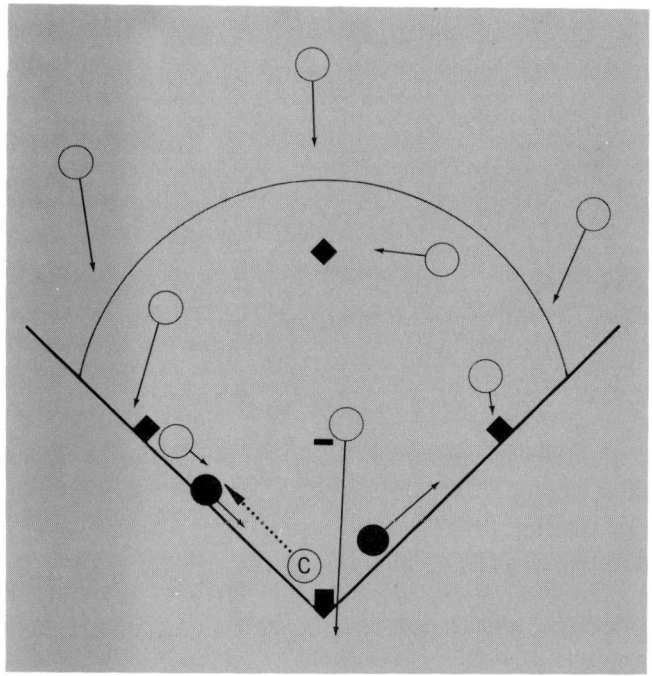

simply to cover home plate, it's likely that Yastrzemski, seeing this, would head back to third.

Thus, Etchebarren charges up the third base line, driving Yastrzemski back, then throws to third baseman Brooks Robinson who makes the tag (A). In order to be able to do this, however, Etchebarren has to get Robinson's cooperation. Robinson must follow Yastrzemski as he breaks for the plate, alert for Etchebarren's throw. Mark Belanger must slant over from his position at shortstop to cover third base. Pitcher Grant Jackson plays a key role, too, for he must dart in to cover home plate; otherwise, Etchebarren must remain there.

5. Healy has two objectives, equal in importance: to catch the ball and hold both runners, which means that (B) is the most likely alternative. As soon as the ball plunks into his glove, Healy checks first base, and if Rudi has broken for second, Healy throws to the second baseman. Shortstop Frank White is a key man. If he sees that Jackson has broken for the plate, he cuts off Healy's throw, and fires the ball to the pitcher, who is covering home plate. If Jackson should stay on third base, however,

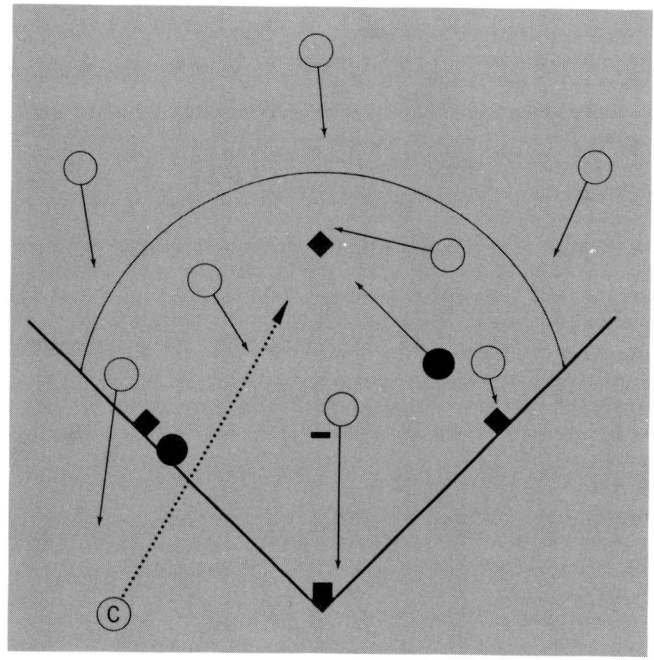

White lets the ball go to second base. Healy, once he's made his throw, hustles to home plate to back up the pitcher.

INDEX

Aaron, Hank, 11
All-Star game, 10
All-Star game selections, 11, 12, 21, 91, 112
Allen, Lee, 75
Allison, Doug, 70
Alomar, Sandy, 118
Alston, Walt, 45, 87
American League, 11, 12, 21, 27, 60, 61, 69, 74, 89, 99, 113
Anaheim Stadium, 115
Anderson, Sparky, 11, 61, 111
Ann Arbor, Michigan, 19
Atlantic Braves, 32

Back-up catcher, 27, 28
Baltimore Orioles, 28, 104, 116
Barney, Rex, 87
Base running, 23, 34, 63, 86, 108
Base stealing, 60, 61, 62, 63, 66, 67, 71, 79, 84, 91
Batting practice, 23, 28, 89, 104
Belanger, Mark, 116, 119
Bell, James (Cool Papa), 89
Bellows Falls, Vermont, 14
Bench, Johnny, 8, 9, 10, 11, 12, 15, 21, 22, 25, 30, 44, 62, 67, 83, 86, 102, 103, 104, 105, 106, 107, 108, 109, 111, 112, 113
Benton, John (Rube), 114
Berra, Yogi, 10, 12, 15, 59, 63, 67, 83, 84, 86, 91, 92, 93, 94, 95, 102
Blocking home plate, 11, 21, 36, 38, 115
Bonds, Bobby, 62
Boone, Bob, 16, 17, 31, 46, 56, 116, 117

Boston Braves, 44, 48
Boston Red Sox, 13, 14, 27, 44, 47, 95, 113, 116
Brainard, Asa, 70
Branca, Ralph, 87
Bresnahan, Roger, 80, 81, 82, 102
Briggs, Walter O., 86
Bristol, Dave, 102
Brock, Lou, 36, 60, 62, 63, 66, 115, 116, 117
Brooklyn Bushwicks, 89
Brooklyn Dodgers, 86, 87, 91, 93, 94, 99, 100, 101
Brown, Bobby, 94
Brown, Mace, 97, 98
Buckner, Bill, 64
Bunts, 11, 34, 61, 62, 94, 116, 118
Busch Stadium, 60
Bushong, A. J. (Doc.), 76

California Angels, 8, 14, 115
Campanaris, Bert, 60
Campanella, Roy, 10, 35, 83, 85, 86, 87, 88, 89, 93, 102
Canton, Ohio, 11
Carlton, Steve, 115
Casanova, Paul, 33
Casey, Hugh, 101
Cash, Norm, 13
Catcher qualifications, 9, 10, 15, 16, 17, 21, 23, 24, 25, 26, 59, 67, 87, 89, 93, 103
Catcher's helmet, 81, 82
Catcher's mitt, 11, 29, 30, 31, 32, 73, 74, 77, 79, 90, 91, 106
Catcher's stance, 34, 67, 70, 71, 77
Cedeno, Cesar, 46, 62

Chadwick, Harry, 73
Chambliss, Chris, 118
Chest protector, 34, 79, 104
Chicago Cubs, 11, 22, 26, 62, 84, 91, 96, 97, 98, 102
Chicago White Sox, 32, 75, 98, 114
Cincinnati, Ohio, 87
Cincinnati Red Stockings, 70
Cincinnati Reds, 9, 11, 15, 26, 38, 62, 63, 79, 83, 86, 100, 102, 103, 104, 107, 109, 111, 113
Clements, Jack, 79
Cleveland Indians, 10, 14, 99
Cochrane, Mickey, 10, 21, 39, 59, 83, 84, 86, 93, 102
Collins, Eddie, 114
Concentration, 25, 93, 115
Cooper, Cecil, 116, 118
Cox, Billy, 94
Crandall, Del, 30, 48, 59
Crawford, Willie, 64
Crosley Field, 100
Cy Young Award, 94, 95

Dark, Alvin, 69
Davidson, Teddy, 9
Dempsey, Rick, 28
Designated hitter, 68, 69
Detroit Tigers, 14, 17, 19, 21, 22, 29, 83, 84, 86
Dickey, Bill, 10, 12, 17, 83, 90, 91, 93, 95, 101, 102
DiMaggio, Joe, 91, 101

Eastern League, 12
Etchebarren, Andy, 116, 118, 119

121

Eugene, Oregon, 16
Ewing William (Buck), 76, 77, 102

Faber, Urban, 114
Face mask, 9, 73, 74, 75, 80, 94, 104, 116
Fairly, Ron, 9
Felsch, Oscar (Happy), 114
Fenway Park, 14, 47
Ferguson, Joe, 17, 18
Fielders' glove, 73, 90
Fingers, Rollie, 109
Fisk, Carlton, 13, 14, 25, 27, 29, 42, 44
Florida Instructional League, 102, 106
Foote, Barry, 21, 22
Ford, Whitey, 42, 43
Fosse, Ray, 9, 10
Freehan, Bill, 17, 19, 20, 21, 22, 29

Gallagher, Alan, 14
Garagiola, Joe, 92
Gehrig, Lou, 90
Gibson, Josh, 89
Giusti, Dave, 15, 107
Glove, hinged, 11, 29, 30; no-break, 11, 29, 30; oversize, 30, 31, 32, 78, 79, 90
Golden Glove Award, 11, 21, 112
Gomez, Lefty, 91
Gordon, Joe, 101
Goslin, Goose, 84
Griffey, Ken, 113
Griffith Stadium, 89
Grote, Jerry, 40, 63, 64

Hadley, Bump, 86
Hague, Joe, 109
Hall of Fame, 42, 75, 77, 81, 91, 93, 98, 100
Haller, Tom, 9
Hano, Arnold, 83
Hargrave, Eugene (Bubbles), 26
Harnett, Charles (Gabby), 10, 83, 93, 95, 96, 97, 98, 102
Healy, Fran, 27, 116, 119
Hegan, Jim, 29, 30
Heinrich, Tommy, 100, 101
Herrmann, Ed, 28, 32, 43
Highland Park, Michigan, 19
Hodges, Gil, 94
Holbert, Bill, 76
Holdsworth, Fred, 14
Home plate, 8, 9, 11, 14, 20, 36, 40, 71, 72, 78, 79, 116, 118, 119
Hough, Charles, 31
Houk, Ralph, 59
Houston Astros, 62
Howard, Elston, 10, 12, 49, 57, 93, 95, 96
Hoyt, Waite, 91
Hubbell, Carl, 100
Humphrey, Terry, 41, 54
Hunt, Ron, 60
Hunter, Jim (Catfish), 43, 48, 49
Huntley, Randy, 11

Injuries, 9, 10, 11, 14, 15, 25, 28, 36, 72, 74, 82, 86, 100, 109
International League, 87, 103
Irvin, Monte, 86

Jackson, Grant, 116, 119
Jackson, Reggie, 60, 109, 116
Javery, Al, 44

Kansas City A's, 98
Kansas City Royals, 27, 59, 116
Keller, Charlie, 101
Kelly, Michael Joseph (King), 75, 77
Kent State, 12
Kingman, Dave, 115, 116
Kissell, George, 16
Kluttz, Clyde, 23, 24
Knuckleball, 30, 31, 32, 63
Koosman, Jerry, 40, 48, 51

Labine, Clem, 94
Larsen, Don, 94
Lee, Loren, 14
Little League, 30
Lombardi, Ernie, 26, 27, 93, 99, 100
Lonborg, Jim, 95
Lopes, Dave, 62
Lopez, Al, 93, 99
Los Angeles Dodgers, 9, 17, 18, 31, 39, 44, 57, 62, 111, 115, 116
Los Angeles *Times*, 17

Mack, Connie, 84
Martin, Pepper, 84
Martinez, Buck, 23
Masi, Phil, 44
Mason, Jim, 118
Mathewson, Christy, 81
Mauch, Gene, 22
May, Milt, 22, 36
McDougald, Gil, 94
McKeon, Jack, 59
McLean, Larry, 38
Memorial Stadium, 116
Menke, Denis, 109
Merchant, Larry, 107
Messersmith, Andy, 39

Milwaukee Braves, 25
Milwaukee Brewers, 22, 30
Minnesota Twins, 47
Minor League, 11, 12, 19, 21, 84, 87, 92, 103
Money, Don, 59
Montreal Expos, 21, 22
Morgan, Joe, 25, 62, 113
Most Valuable Player, 26, 84, 86, 92, 95, 97, 104, 112
Munson, Thurman, 11, 12, 14, 25, 26, 29, 35, 116, 118
Murcer, Bobby, 47

Naismith, Dr. James, 74
National Association, 76
National League, 9, 26, 27, 30, 61, 62, 74, 76, 92, 94, 99
National League Eastern Division, 107
Negro All-Star team, 87
Negro National League, 89
Nettles, Graig, 116, 118
New York Actives, 74
New York Giants, 76, 81, 82, 86, 100, 114
New York Metropolitans, 76
New York Mets, 26, 30, 31, 40, 48, 63, 64, 94, 95, 111, 115
New York Times, The, 76
New York Yankees, 11, 12, 17, 23, 28, 42, 43, 49, 57, 62, 86, 90, 91, 93, 94, 95, 100, 111, 115
Newark Bears, 94
Newcombe, Don, 87, 91, 94
Nicetown Athletic Club, Philadelphia, 87
Niekro, Phil, 32
North, Bill, 60, 62

Oakland A's, 9, 10, 43, 60, 62, 67, 69, 74, 94, 107, 109, 116
Oates, Bob, 17
O'Connor, John (Rowdy Jack), 79
Old Timers' Day, 88
Oliva, Tony, 47
O'Rourke, Jim, 74, 75, 77, 102
Owen, Mickey, 100, 101

Pacific Coast League, 84
Page, Ted, 89
Pennock, Herb, 91
Perez, Tony, 106, 109
Philadelphia Athletics, 39, 83, 84
Philadelphia Phillies, 16, 31, 46, 79, 115
Pittsburgh Keystones, 79
Pittsburgh Pirates, 14, 15, 44, 53, 68, 97, 98, 107, 113
Polo Grounds, 81, 114
Pop flies, 35, 36, 96
Porter, Darrell, 22, 30, 49
Portland Beavers, 84
Powers, Jimmy, 96

Rader, Dave, 22, 34
Raffensberger, Ken, 86
Raleigh-Durham, 16
Rariden, Bill, 114, 115
Rau, Doug, 45
Reserve rule, 75
Reynolds, Allie, 91
Rivers, Mickey, 115, 116
Robinson, Brooks, 104, 119
Robinson, Frank, 14
Robinson, Jackie, 89
Rodriguez, Eliseo (Ellie), 2
Rookie of the Year, 10, 12, 14, 103
Rose, Pete, 10, 25, 46, 106, 109

Rudi, Joe, 116, 119
Ruffing, Red, 91
Ruth, Babe, 89, 90, 97
Ruthven, Dick, 60
Ryan, Noland, 10, 48

St. Louis Cardinals, 15, 25, 51, 60, 84, 92, 115
San Francisco Giants, 22, 34, 38, 47
Sanguillen, Manuel (Manny), 14, 15, 68
Schalk, Ray, 93, 98, 99
Scouts, 23, 24, 25, 27
Seaver, Tom, 48, 57, 63, 64, 115, 117
Seminick, Andy, 16
Shea Stadium, 31, 115
Shinguards, 79, 80, 81, 102, 104, 115
Signal system, 46, 47, 48, 49, 53, 54, 55, 56, 57, 66, 73, 75
Simmons, Ted, 15, 16
Simpson, O. J., 10
Sizemore, Ted, 63, 66
Sliding, 9, 38, 64
Smith, Reggie, 51, 115, 116
Spalding, A. G. Company, 77, 79
Sport Magazine, 83
Sporting News, The, 14, 103
Spring training, 14
Stanford University, 16
Stargell, Willie, 53
Staub, Daniel (Rusty), 25
Stengel, Casey, 44
Substitution rule, 75, 76
Sundberg, Jim, 22
Sutton, Don, 39

Swisher, Steve, 22
Switch hitter, 15, 16

Tagging base runners, 8, 10, 13, 38, 119
Target area, 49, 50, 56
Tenace, Gene, 81, 116
Texas Rangers, 22
Tiant, Luis, 44
Tolan, Bobby, 106
Torre, Joe, 16, 25, 115, 116, 117
Troy Haymakers, 76
Tyng, Fred, 73

Umpires, 42, 67, 77
University of Michigan, 19

Walberg, Rube, 39
Walker, Tom, 41
Washington, Herb, 60, 67, 69
Washington *Post,* 89
Weaver, Earl, 28, 116
White, Frank, 119
Wild pitch, 9
Wills, Maury, 62, 63
Wilson, Jimmie, 84, 93
Woods, Wilbur, 32

World Series, 14, 81, 84, 91, 93, 94, 97, 100, 104, 107, 111, 113, 114, 115
Wright, Harry, 70
Wrigley Field, 97

Yankee Stadium, 89
Yastrzemski, Carl, 14, 46, 47, 117, 118, 119
Yeager, Steve, 17, 18, 31, 32, 45, 57, 115, 117

Zimmerman, Henry (Heinie), 114